2013

The State of
Food Insecurity in the World

The multiple dimensions of food security

FOOD AND AGRICULTURE ORGANIZATION OF THE UNITED NATIONS
Rome, 2013

Required citation:
FAO, IFAD and WFP. 2013. *The State of Food Insecurity in the World 2013.*
The multiple dimensions of food security. Rome, FAO.

ISBN 978-92-5-107916-4 (print)
E-ISBN 978-92-5-107917-1 (PDF)

CONTENTS

Thirteen years ago, world leaders came together to adopt the United Nations Millennium Declaration. They committed their nations to a new global partnership to reduce extreme poverty and hunger, setting out a series of targets to be met by 2015, which have become known as the Millennium Development Goals (MDGs). These goals express the world's commitment to improve the lives of billions of people and to address development challenges.

Under MDG 1, which aims to eradicate extreme poverty and hunger, the world sought to halve, between 1990 and 2015, the proportion of people who suffer from hunger. With only two years remaining, 38 countries have reached this target, 18 of which have also achieved the even more stringent goal, established during the 1996 World Food Summit (WFS) in Rome, of halving the absolute number of hungry in the same time period.

These successes demonstrate that, with political commitment, effective institutions, good policies, a comprehensive approach and adequate levels of investment, we can win the fight against hunger and poverty, a necessary first step to arrive at the other development milestones set by the MDGs.

As with every edition, the 2013 report of *The State of Food Insecurity in the World* updates progress towards the MDG and WFS hunger goals: globally, by region and by individual country. For developing regions as a whole, the latest assessment suggests that further progress has been made towards the 2015 MDG target. The same progress, assessed against the more ambitious WFS goal, obviously appears much more modest. A total of 842 million people, or 12 percent of the world's population, were experiencing chronic hunger in 2011–13, 26 million fewer than the number reported last year and down from 1 015 million in 1990–92.

The updated assessment also suggests that the MDG 2015 hunger goal remains within reach. With new estimates for the entire MDG horizon, the starting level for undernourishment in the 1990–92 base year was 23.6 percent in developing regions, implying an MDG target of 11.8 percent for 2015. Assuming that the average annual decline over the past 21 years continues to 2015, the prevalence of undernourishment in developing regions would approach 13 percent, a share slightly above the MDG target. With a final push in the next couple of years, we can still reach it.

The 2013 report goes beyond measuring chronic food deprivation. It presents a broader suite of indicators that aims to capture the multidimensional nature of food insecurity, its determinants and outcomes. This suite, compiled for every country, allows a more nuanced picture of their food security status, guiding policy-makers in the design and implementation of targeted and effective policy measures that can contribute to the eradication of hunger, food insecurity and malnutrition.

Drawing on the suite of indicators, the report also examines the diverse experiences of six countries. These experiences show that other forms of malnutrition can sometimes be more significant than undernourishment. In such circumstances, policy interventions to improve food security need to include nutrition-sensitive interventions in agriculture and the food system as a whole, as well as in public health and education, especially of women. Nutrition-focused social protection may need to target the most vulnerable, including pregnant women, adolescent girls and children.

Policies aimed at enhancing agricultural productivity and increasing food availability, especially when smallholders are targeted, can achieve hunger reduction even where poverty is widespread. When they are combined with social protection and other measures that increase the incomes of poor families, they can have an even more positive effect and spur rural development, by creating vibrant markets and employment opportunities, resulting in equitable economic growth.

Not surprisingly, the specific country experiences suggest that high poverty levels generally go hand in hand with high levels of undernourishment. But undernourishment can also be more severe than poverty, especially when both are at high levels. As food is one of the most income-responsive of all basic necessities, higher incomes can therefore expedite reductions in undernourishment.

Ultimately, political stability, effective governance and, most importantly, uninterrupted long-term commitments to mainstreaming food security and nutrition in policies and programmes are key to the reduction of hunger and malnutrition. FAO, IFAD and WFP are committed to keeping food security high on the development agenda and ensuring that it is firmly embedded in the post-2015 vision currently being developed. They must be supported and sustained by improvements in agriculture and in the investment climate, twinned with social protection. Only then will we be able to reach well beyond the MDG targets to achieve major reductions in poverty and undernourishment.

José Graziano da Silva
FAO Director-General

Kanayo F. Nwanze
IFAD President

Ertharin Cousin
WFP Executive Director

ACKNOWLEDGEMENTS

The State of Food Insecurity in the World 2013 was prepared under the overall leadership of Jomo Kwame Sundaram, Assistant-Director-General, and the guidance of the management team of the FAO Economic and Social Development Department.

Technical coordination of the publication was carried out by Pietro Gennari, with additional contributions from Kostas Stamoulis. Piero Conforti, George Rapsomanikis and Josef Schmidhuber served as technical editors. Michelle Kendrick provided coordination for the editorial, graphics, layout and publishing services.

This is the third edition of this report that has been jointly prepared by FAO, the International Fund for Agricultural Development (IFAD) and the World Food Programme (WFP). Alessandra Garbero and Sónia Gonçalves, of IFAD, Joyce Luma and Astrid Mathiassen, of WFP, collaborated in preparing the country case studies. Alessandra Garbero and Joyce Luma coordinated support from their respective institutions. Carlos Seré and Thomas Elhaut (IFAD) and Lisa Hjelm, Issa Sanogo, John McHarris, Fillippo Pompili and Simeon Hollema (WFP) provided valuable inputs.

The section on *Undernourishment around the world in 2013* was prepared by the Statistics Division (ESS) of the Economic and Social Development Department, with key technical contributions from Piero Conforti, Josef Schmidhuber, Carlo Cafiero, Adam Prakash, Nathalie Troubat, Franck Cachia and Pietro Gennari.

The section on *Measuring different dimensions of food security* was prepared by Piero Conforti and Josef Schmidhuber, with substantive inputs from Pietro Gennari, Nathalie Troubat, Andrea Borlizzi, Adam Prakash and Michael Kao. The box on "A monitoring framework for the post-2015 development agenda" was prepared by Pietro Gennari.

The section on *Food security dimensions at the national level* was prepared by George Rapsomanikis, Jelle Bruinsma and MarieJo Cortijo, all of the Agricultural Development Economics Division (ESA) of the Economic and Social Development Department; Alessandra Garbero and Sónia Gonçalves (IFAD); and Joyce Luma and Astrid Mathiassen (WFP). Analysis for this section was kindly provided by Federica Alfani, Natalia Merkusheva and Giulia Ponzini.

Cinzia Cerri was responsible for preparing Annex 1 and the related data preparation and processing. Pietro Gennari and Carlo Cafiero produced Annex 2. Jelle Bruinsma compiled Annex 3. Chiara Brunelli, Nathan Wanner, Firas Yassin, Andrea Borlizzi and Nathalie Troubat also provided excellent technical input and data processing.

Valuable comments and suggestions were provided by Terri Ballard, Jelle Bruinsma, Carlo Cafiero, Vili Fuavao, Juan Carlos García y Cebolla, Panagiotis Karfakis, Tomasz Lonc, Árni Mathiesen, Eva Müller, Abdessalam Ould Ahmed, Rodrigo Rivera, Sanginboy Sanginov, Ramesh Sharma, Salar Tayyib, James Tefft, Nathalie Troubat, Keith Wiebe and Xiangjun Yao. Abdolreza Abbassian, Gladys Moreno Garcia, Adam Prakash and Nicolas Sakoff provided useful background material.

Copy-editing and proofreading services were provided by Paul Neate and graphic design and layout services were provided by Flora DiCarlo. Printing services were coordinated by the Meeting Programming and Documentation Service of the FAO Conference, Council and Protocol Affairs Division.

Undernourishment around the world in 2013

Progress continues…

FAO's most recent estimates indicate that, globally, 842 million people – 12 percent of the global population – were unable to meet their dietary energy requirements in 2011–13, down from 868 million reported for the 2010–12 period in last year's report. Thus, around one in eight people in the world are likely to have suffered from chronic hunger, not having enough food for an active and healthy life. The vast majority of hungry people – 827 million of them – live in developing regions, where the prevalence of undernourishment is now estimated at 14.3 percent in 2011–13 (Table 1).

TABLE 1

Undernourishment around the world, 1990–92 to 2011–13

	Number of undernourished (*millions*) and prevalence (%) of undernourishment				
	1990–92	2000–2002	2005–07	2008–10	2011–13*
WORLD	1 015.3	957.3	906.6	878.2	842.3
	18.9%	*15.5%*	*13.8%*	*12.9%*	*12.0%*
DEVELOPED REGIONS	19.8	18.4	13.6	15.2	15.7
	<5%	*<5%*	*<5%*	*<5%*	*<5%*
DEVELOPING REGIONS	995.5	938.9	892.9	863.0	826.6
	23.6%	*18.8%*	*16.7%*	*15.5%*	*14.3%*
Africa	177.6	214.3	217.6	226.0	226.4
	27.3%	*25.9%*	*23.4%*	*22.7%*	*21.2%*
Northern Africa	4.6	4.9	4.8	4.4	3.7
	<5%	*<5%*	*<5%*	*<5%*	*<5%*
Sub-Saharan Africa	173.1	209.5	212.8	221.6	222.7
	32.7%	*30.6%*	*27.5%*	*26.6%*	*24.8%*
Asia	751.3	662.3	619.6	585.5	552.0
	24.1%	*18.3%*	*16.1%*	*14.7%*	*13.5%*
Caucasus and Central Asia	9.7	11.6	7.3	7.0	5.5
	14.4%	*16.2%*	*9.8%*	*9.2%*	*7.0%*
Eastern Asia	278.7	193.5	184.8	169.1	166.6
	22.2%	*14.0%*	*13.0%*	*11.7%*	*11.4%*
South-Eastern Asia	140.3	113.6	94.2	80.5	64.5
	31.1%	*21.5%*	*16.8%*	*13.8%*	*10.7%*
Southern Asia	314.3	330.2	316.6	309.9	294.7
	25.7%	*22.2%*	*19.7%*	*18.5%*	*16.8%*
Western Asia	8.4	13.5	16.8	19.1	20.6
	6.6%	*8.3%*	*9.2%*	*9.7%*	*9.8%*
Latin America and the Caribbean	65.7	61.0	54.6	50.3	47.0
	14.7%	*11.7%*	*9.8%*	*8.7%*	*7.9%*
Caribbean	8.3	7.2	7.5	6.8	7.2
	27.6%	*21.3%*	*21.0%*	*18.8%*	*19.3%*
Latin America	57.4	53.8	47.2	43.5	39.8
	13.8%	*11.0%*	*9.0%*	*8.0%*	*7.1%*
Oceania	0.8	1.2	1.1	1.1	1.2
	13.5%	*16.0%*	*12.8%*	*11.8%*	*12.1%*

Note: * Projections.
Source: FAO.

…but is insufficient overall to achieve the hunger reduction goals

While the estimated number of undernourished people has continued to decrease, the rate of progress appears insufficient to reach international goals for hunger reduction. There are two established targets against which progress in reducing hunger is assessed. One is the 1996 World Food Summit (WFS) target, which is to halve the number of hungry people; the other is the 2001 Millennium Development Goal (MDG) hunger target, which is to halve the proportion of hungry people in the total population. Both targets have 1990 as the starting year and 2015 as the target year. Given the often high rates of population growth in many hunger-affected countries, the WFS target is the more ambitious goal. The deviation of actual progress from the target trajectory is therefore growing more rapidly for the WFS target than for the MDG one, at least for developing regions as a whole (Figure 1). To meet the WFS target, the number of hungry people in developing regions would have to be reduced to 498 million by 2015, a goal that is out of reach at the global level. However, many individual countries are on track to meet the WFS target: indeed, 18 countries[1]* had already met it in 2012 and received a special recognition during the 2013 FAO Conference.

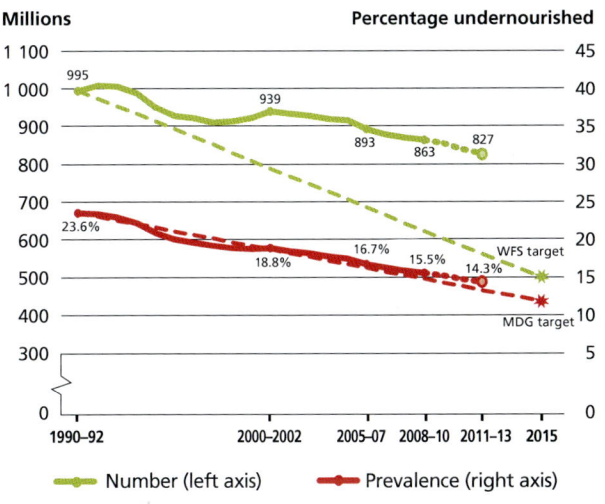

FIGURE 1

Undernourishment in the developing regions: actual progress and target achievement trajectories towards the MDG and WFS targets

Number (left axis)   Prevalence (right axis)

Note: Data for 2011–13 in all graphics refer to provisional estimates.
Source: FAO.

The MDG target could still be reached, but more efforts are needed

The MDG hunger target of halving the proportion of people who are undernourished is less ambitious than the WFS target, and the deviation from its trajectory appears relatively small (Figure 1). The current assessment pegs undernourishment in developing regions at around 24 percent of the population in 1990–92, thus implying an MDG target of 12 percent. Assuming that the average annual decline over the past 21 years continues to 2015, the prevalence of undernourishment in developing regions would be 13 percent, marginally above the MDG target. Nevertheless, the target can be met, provided that additional efforts to reduce hunger are brought underway, both to address immediate needs and to sustain longer-term progress.

---

* All notes and references are provided at the end of the report, see pages 51–52.

As the target year is fast approaching, there is a need for programmes that deliver quick results. Measures to improve access to food through safety nets and similar interventions can do this. They also promise to have longer-lasting positive effects on food availability by raising local demand, thus stimulating food production. Such programmes include, *inter alia*, cash transfers and cash-and-voucher schemes. Initial results of these programmes suggest that they can lead not only to higher consumption, but also to increased investments in agricultural assets, including farm implements and livestock, and more food from own production. There is also evidence that such programmes can create significant income multiplier effects through trade and production linkages. Over the longer term, they can generate positive feedback whereby demand created through safety nets stimulates smallholder food production and thus helps both poor consumers and producers. These programmes lie at the heart of the twin-track approach to reducing hunger, stimulating food demand, which, in turn, provides incentives to increase production and more income-generating opportunities for smallholder production.

To sustain their longer-term viability, demand-enhancing efforts need to be supplemented by effective supply-side measures. This is particularly important when hunger reduction programmes aim to reach large rural populations in the absence of adequate physical and institutional infrastructure. The 2012 edition of *The State of Food and Agriculture* made a powerful case for investing in agriculture to reduce poverty and hunger. It showed that investing in agriculture contributes strongly to increasing food security, which in turn helps promote economic diversification and growth. Increased agricultural productivity generates higher incomes and creates income-generating opportunities for otherwise destitute population groups, offering a recognized way to escape the poverty trap in many rural areas.

Large differences in hunger persist across regions

Africa remains the region with the highest prevalence of undernourishment, with around one in four people estimated to be undernourished. Levels and trends in undernourishment differ within the continent. While sub-Saharan Africa has the highest prevalence of under-nourishment, there has been some improvement over the last two decades, with the prevalence of under-nourishment declining from 32.7 percent to 24.8 percent. Northern Africa, by contrast, is characterized by a much lower prevalence of undernourishment and by much faster progress than sub-Saharan Africa. Overall, the region is not on track to achieve the MDG hunger target, reflecting too little progress in both parts of the continent (Figure 2).

Both the number and proportion of people undernourished have decreased significantly in most countries in Asia, particularly in South-Eastern Asia, but progress in Southern Asia has been slower, especially in terms of the number of people undernourished. The prevalence of undernourishment is lower in Western Asia than in other parts of the region but has risen steadily since 1990–92. With a decline in prevalence from 31.1 to 10.7 percent, the most rapid progress was recorded in South-Eastern Asia, followed by Eastern Asia. The Asia region as a whole is nearly on track to achieve the MDG hunger target. The MDG target has already been reached in the Caucasus and Central Asia, East Asia and South-Eastern Asia, while it has nearly been reached in Latin America and the Caribbean (Figure 3).

FIGURE **2**

Regions differ markedly in progress towards achieving the MDG and WFS hunger targets

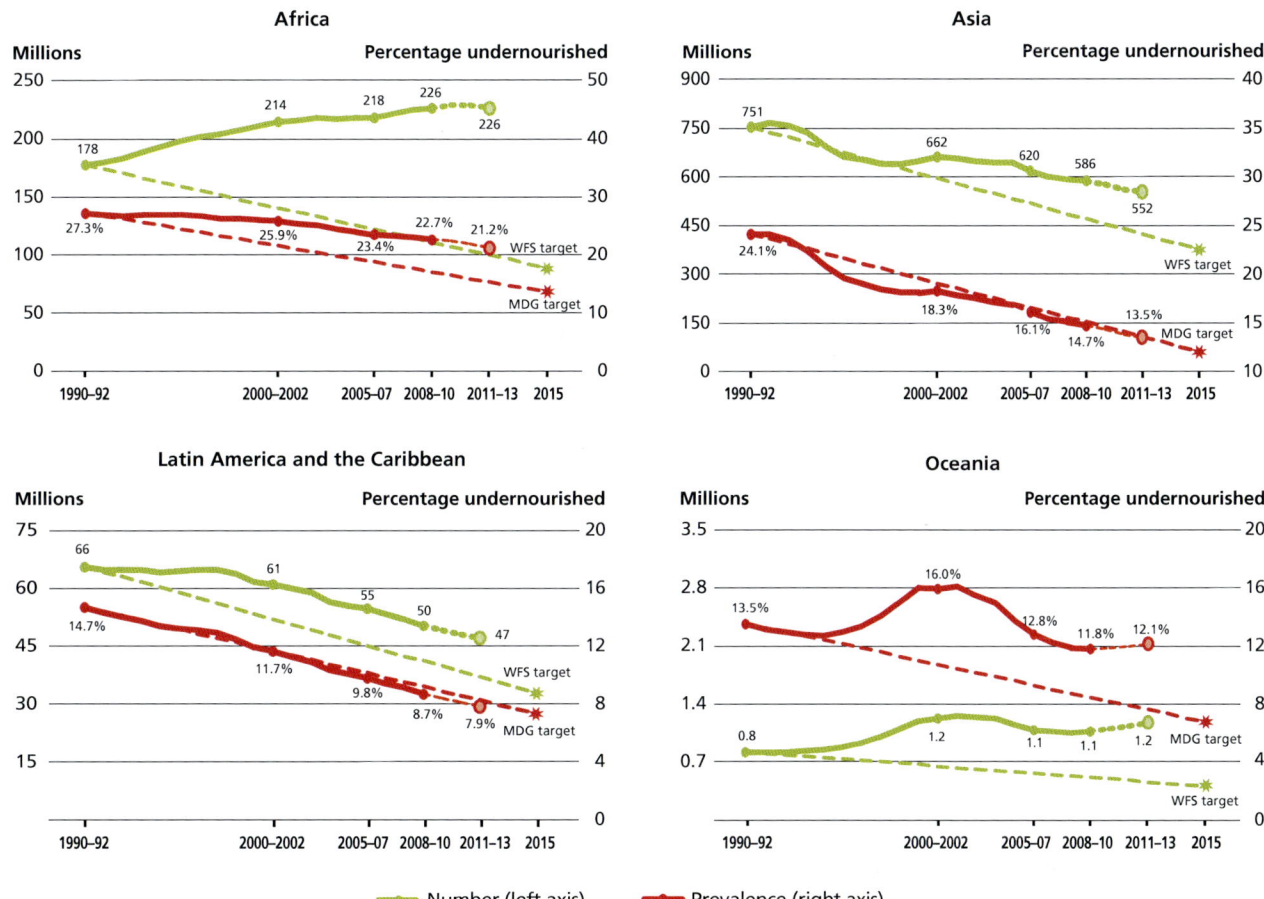

Source: FAO.

FIGURE **3**

Undernourishment trends: progress made in almost all regions, but at very different rates

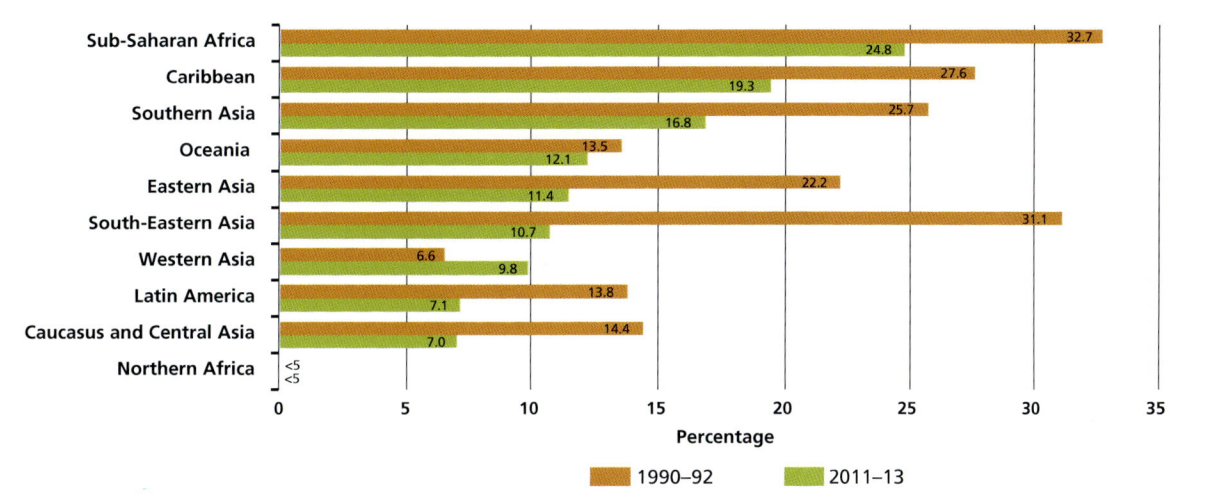

Source: FAO.

Why do hunger trends differ across regions?

Progress in reducing hunger reflects country and regional specificities in terms of economic conditions, infrastructure, the organization of food production, the presence of social provisions and political and institutional stability. In Western Asia, the worsening undernourishment trend appears to be mostly related to food price inflation and political instability. In Northern Africa, where progress has been slow, the same factors are relevant. Lack of natural resources, especially good-quality cropland and renewable water resources, also limit the regions' food production potential. Meeting the food needs of these regions' rapidly growing populations has been possible only through importing large quantities of cereals. Some of these cereal imports are financed by petroleum exports; simply put, these regions export hydrocarbons and import carbohydrates to ensure their food security. Both food and energy are made more affordable domestically through large, untargeted subsidies.

The regions' dependency on food imports and oil exports make them susceptible to price swings on world commodity markets. The most precarious food security situations arise in countries where proceeds from hydrocarbon exports have slowed or stalled, food subsidies are circumscribed by growing fiscal deficits or civil unrest has disrupted domestic food chains.

While at the global level there has been an overall reduction in the number of undernourished between 1990–92 and 2011–13 (Figure 4), different rates of progress across regions have led to changes in the distribution of undernourished people in the world. Most of the world's undernourished people are still to be found in Southern Asia, closely followed by sub-Saharan Africa and Eastern Asia. The regional share has declined most in Eastern Asia and South-Eastern Asia, and to a lesser extent in Latin America and the Caribbean and in the Caucasus and Central Asia. Meanwhile, the share has increased in Southern Asia, in sub-Saharan Africa and in Western Asia and Northern Africa.

Many countries have experienced higher economic growth over the last few years, a key reason for progress in hunger reduction. Still, growth does not reach its potential, owing to structural constraints. Arguably the most

FIGURE 4

The changing distribution of hunger in the world
Number and share of undernourished by region, 1990–92 and 2011–13

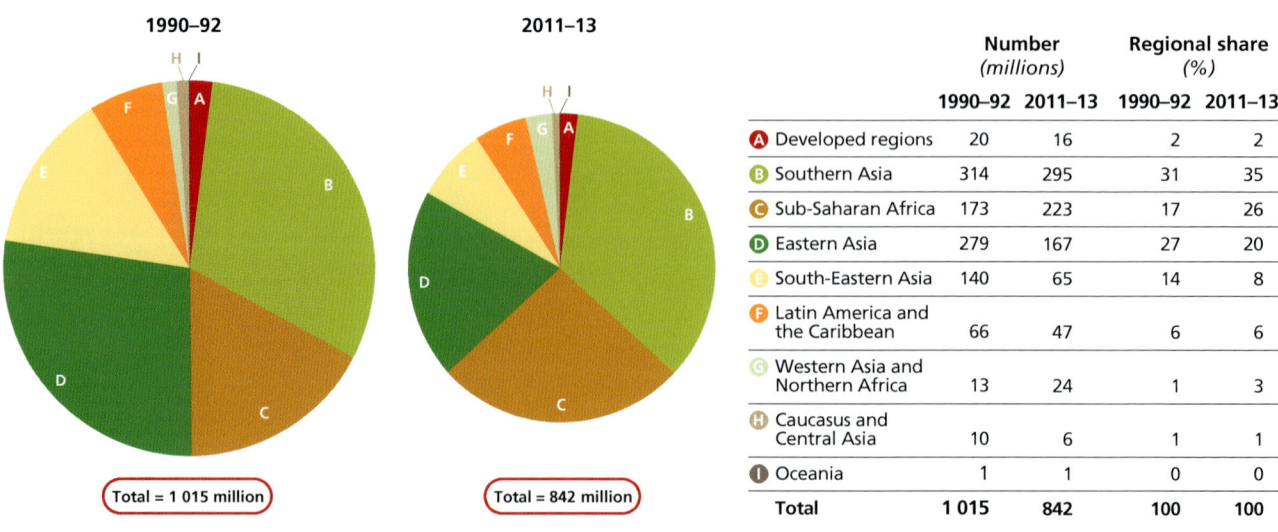

		Number (millions)		Regional share (%)	
		1990–92	2011–13	1990–92	2011–13
Ⓐ	Developed regions	20	16	2	2
Ⓑ	Southern Asia	314	295	31	35
Ⓒ	Sub-Saharan Africa	173	223	17	26
Ⓓ	Eastern Asia	279	167	27	20
Ⓔ	South-Eastern Asia	140	65	14	8
Ⓕ	Latin America and the Caribbean	66	47	6	6
Ⓖ	Western Asia and Northern Africa	13	24	1	3
Ⓗ	Caucasus and Central Asia	10	6	1	1
Ⓘ	Oceania	1	1	0	0
	Total	**1 015**	**842**	**100**	**100**

1990–92   Total = 1 015 million

2011–13   Total = 842 million

Note: The areas of the pie charts are proportional to the total number of undernourished in each period. All figures are rounded.
Source: FAO.

important is the often woefully inadequate infrastructure that plagues vast areas of rural Africa. Much improved communication and broader access to information technology may, to some extent, have helped overcome traditional infrastructure constraints, and promoted market integration. Also encouraging is the pick-up in agricultural productivity growth, buttressed by increased public investment, incentives generated by higher food prices and renewed interest of private investors in agriculture. In some countries, remittance inflows from migrants have helped spur domestic growth. Remittances have increased small-scale investment, which was particularly beneficial to growth where food production and distribution still rely on small-scale and local networks. This holds in particular for sub-Saharan African countries, where a combination of higher crop yields and increased livestock production have led to a reduction of undernourishment.

Many countries in Eastern Asia have benefited from continuous and often rapid economic growth. In general,

they were less affected by the economic slow-downs that engulfed many other developing countries in the past decade and member countries of the Organisation for Economic Co-operation and Development (OECD) in the late 2000s. Countries in South-Eastern Asia have shown considerable inflows of remittances from the West and some oil-rich countries in Western Asia. These transfers have often driven small-scale investment in sectors such as agriculture and construction. Robust income growth, in conjunction with relatively high income responsiveness on the demand side and policies to increase agricultural productivity, has helped reduce the undernourishment burden in these regions.

Similar factors seem to explain the good progress recorded by most countries in Latin America and the Caribbean. Economic growth, political and institutional stability, incentives to raise agricultural productivity and overall economic development have been the main sources of progress.

What was the impact of price volatility observed over recent years?

The evolution of the prevalence of undernourishment estimates capture trends in chronic hunger. Because of the characteristics of the data on which it is based, the prevalence of undernourishment indicator does not reflect acute, short-term changes in malnutrition resulting from short-term changes in the economic environment. The large swings in primary food prices observed since 2008, often measured by the FAO Food Price Index (FPI), are a prominent example of such short-term shocks. Price and income swings affect the food security of poor and hungry people more than the steady trend in the prevalence of under-nourishment suggests. But recent data on global and regional food consumer price indices (food CPIs) suggest that food price hikes at the primary commodity level generally have little effect on consumer prices and that the swings in consumer prices were much more muted than those faced by agricultural producers or recorded in international trade.

Overall, the new data on food prices at the consumer level give rise to two basic findings.

The first is that increases in the FPI translate into higher consumer prices only to a very limited degree and with a time lag of a few months. The lag in transmission from international prices (as captured by the FPI) to consumer prices (food CPI) is explained, in large measure, by the time

needed to harvest, ship and then process primary products into final food items for consumers. The lag is highlighted if the two indicators are plotted on different scales (Figure 5, left). The limited transmission is explained by a combination of factors that determine vertical price transmission in every food economy, including mark-ups for transportation, processing and marketing, and by any subsidies at the consumer level. The limited nature of this price transmission is well illustrated by plotting both indicators on the same scale (Figure 5, right).

The second finding is that regional differences in price transmission are surprisingly small. This means that, even in regions characterized by short supply chains and high levels of subsistence production, changes in producer prices of primary products have only a limited effect on final consumer prices (Figure 6). The only noticeable exception is Eastern Africa, where price transmission is high and consumers have been exposed more fully to swings in prices of primary food products. This is also the case for low-income, food-importing countries, in which poor consumers may allocate more than 75 percent of their expenditure to food; in these countries, increases in producer prices can significantly reduce the ability of consumers to meet their food needs.

FIGURE 5

Changes in local consumer food prices lag behind changes in international producer prices and are much smaller

Source: FAO.

FIGURE 6

Global Food Price Index and regional consumer price indices

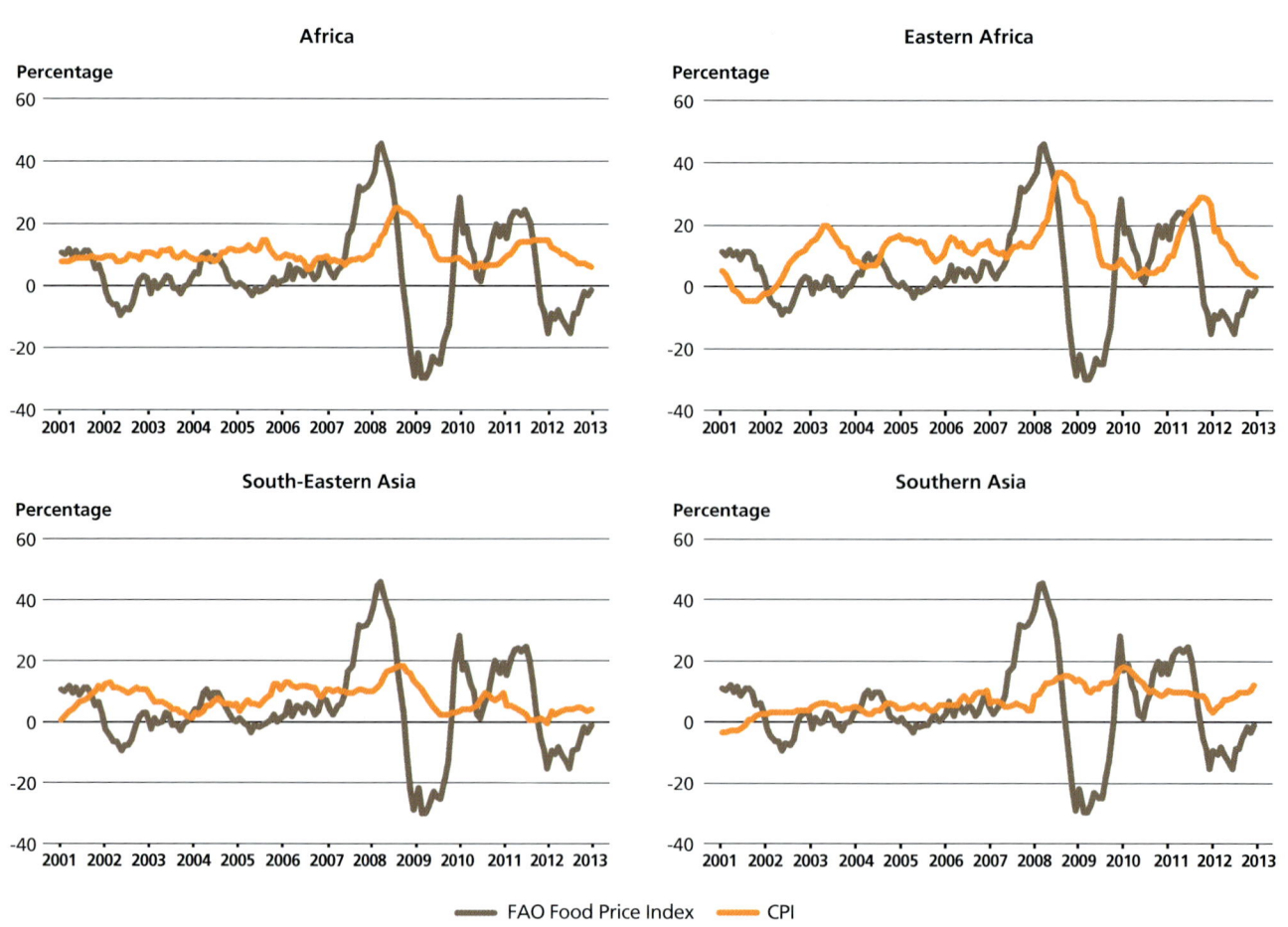

Source: FAO.

In addition, the impact of price swings on under-nourishment can be reduced by consumers switching between food items. When prices rise, consumers often shift from more expensive and more nutritious foodstuffs to less-expensive but often also less-nutritious foods. While this allows consumers to maintain their dietary energy intake, it heightens the risk of other forms of malnutrition, such as micronutrient deficiencies. Consuming less nutritious food can have adverse long-term effects on food utilization, resulting in undernutrition (see *Annex 3: Glossary of selected terms used in this report* for definitions of these terms).

People's health and productivity can also be impaired. These changes, however, are unlikely to be captured by the prevalence of undernourishment indicator: almost unchanged prevalence of undernourishment can mask changes in other forms of malnutrition. This underlines the complexity of food security, and the need for a comprehensive approach to its measurement. The next section will discuss such an approach, and present a suite of indicators that captures more fully the various causes or determinants of food security, as well as its manifestations or outcomes.

Key messages

- **A total of 842 million people in 2011–13, or around one in eight people in the world, were estimated to be suffering from chronic hunger, regularly not getting enough food to conduct an active life. This figure is lower than the 868 million reported with reference to 2010–12. The total number of undernourished has fallen by 17 percent since 1990–92.**

- **Developing regions as a whole have registered significant progress towards the MDG 1 hunger target. If the average annual decline of the past 21 years continues to 2015, the prevalence of undernourishment will reach a level close to the target. Meeting it would require considerable and immediate additional efforts.**

- **Growth can raise incomes and reduce hunger, but higher economic growth may not reach everyone. It may not lead to more and better jobs for all, unless policies specifically target the poor, especially those in rural areas. In poor countries, hunger and poverty reduction will only be achieved with growth that is not only sustained, but also broadly shared.**

- **Despite overall progress, marked differences across regions persist. Sub-Saharan Africa remains the region with the highest prevalence of undernourishment, with modest progress in recent years. Western Asia shows no progress, while Southern Asia and Northern Africa show slow progress. Significant reductions in both the number of people who are undernourished and the prevalence of undernourishment have occurred in most countries of Eastern and South-Eastern Asia, as well as in Latin America.**

- **Price and income swings can significantly affect the poor and hungry. However, recent data on global and regional food consumer price indices suggest that price hikes in primary food markets had a limited effect on consumer prices, and that price swings in consumer prices were more muted than those faced by producers. When prices rise, however, consumers often shift to cheaper, less-nutritious foods, heightening the risks of micronutrient deficiencies and other forms of malnutrition, which can have long-term adverse effects on people's health, development and productivity.**

Measuring different dimensions of food security

The preceding section discussed food security in terms of the prevalence of undernourishment indicator, which is a measure of dietary energy deprivation. As a standalone indicator, the prevalence of undernourishment indicator is not able to capture the complexity and multidimensionality of food security, as defined by the 2009 Declaration of the World Summit on Food Security: *"Food security exists when all people, at all times, have physical, social and economic access to sufficient, safe and nutritious food, which meets their*

FOOD SECURITY INDICATORS	DIMENSION	
Average dietary energy supply adequacy Average value of food production Share of dietary energy supply derived from cereals, roots and tubers Average protein supply Average supply of protein of animal origin	AVAILABILITY	STATIC and DYNAMIC DETERMINANTS
Percentage of paved roads over total roads Road density Rail lines density	PHYSICAL ACCESS	
Domestic food price index	ECONOMIC ACCESS	
Access to improved water sources Access to improved sanitation facilities	UTILIZATION	
Cereal import dependency ratio Percentage of arable land equipped for irrigation Value of food imports over total merchandise exports	VULNERABILITY	
Political stability and absence of violence/terrorism Domestic food price volatility Per capita food production variability Per capita food supply variability	SHOCKS	
Prevalence of undernourishment Share of food expenditure of the poor Depth of the food deficit Prevalence of food inadequacy	ACCESS	OUTCOMES
Percentage of children under 5 years of age affected by wasting Percentage of children under 5 years of age who are stunted Percentage of children under 5 years of age who are underweight Percentage of adults who are underweight Prevalence of anaemia among pregnant women Prevalence of anaemia among children under 5 years of age Prevalence of vitamin A deficiency (forthcoming) Prevalence of iodine deficiency (forthcoming)	UTILIZATION	

Note: Values and detailed descriptions and metadata for these indicators are available on the companion website (www.fao.org/publications/sofi/en/).
Source: FAO.

dietary needs and food preferences for an active and healthy life."[2]

Based on this definition, four food security dimensions can be identified: food availability, economic and physical access to food, food utilization and stability (vulnerability and shocks) over time. Each food security dimension is described by specific indicators. Figure 7 provides an overview of the suite of indicators and their organization into the four dimensions of food security.

Measuring the complexity of food security is part of a broader debate that currently takes place in the preparation process of the post-2015 development agenda. These broader measurement challenges, as well as the processes under way and the new proposals for food security monitoring, are summarized in Box 1.

BOX **1**

A monitoring framework for the post-2015 development agenda

Beyond the MDGs
A new global development agenda for the period beyond 2015 is currently being shaped. One major international forum driving this process is the 30-member Open Working Group on Sustainable Development Goals, established by the General Assembly of the United Nations (UN) on 22 January 2013. The Group will deliver a proposal to be considered by the General Assembly in September 2014. Meanwhile, the High-Level Panel of Eminent Persons on the Post-2015 Development Agenda, appointed in July 2012 by the UN Secretary-General, delivered its report on the post-2015 development agenda on 30 May 2013.[1] The UN system has been contributing to the definition of the post-2015 agenda through the UN System Task Team on the Post-2015 UN Development Agenda.

One lesson that has emerged from the current discussions of the development agenda is the need to improve monitoring. Good monitoring requires a combination of approaches, and the ability to produce regular updates of indicators. The new monitoring system should combine monitoring of human development – "people-focused" metrics – and of the resource base, its use and related stresses – "planet-focused" indicators. A link between these two sets of metrics should be embedded in the design of the new monitoring system at the outset. Data can be collected through a combination of periodic in-depth surveys and lighter, flexible and more frequent experience-based surveys (in which respondents self-report on their experiences).

The three Rome-based agencies (FAO, IFAD and WFP) are well positioned to contribute to the post-2015 development agenda. Their work programmes are largely inspired by the Zero Hunger Challenge proposed by the UN Secretary-General. As emphasized in the recent report of the High-Level Panel (p. 30), this has five targets:

- *end hunger and protect the right of everyone to access sufficient, safe, affordable, and nutritious food;*
- *reduce stunting by x%, wasting by y%, and anaemia by z% for all children under five;*
- *increase agricultural productivity by x%, with a focus on sustainably increasing smallholder yields and access to irrigation;*
- *adopt sustainable agricultural and ocean and freshwater fishery practices and rebuild designated fish stocks to sustainable levels; and*
- *reduce postharvest loss and food waste by x%.*

The Panel emphasized sustainability as a necessary basis for efforts aimed at building lasting prosperity for youth. The Panel also advocates a "data revolution" for sustainable development, noting the potential of open and accessible data to contribute to sustainable development and the need to use non-traditional data sources (e.g. crowd sourcing). The report also stresses the need to disaggregate data by gender, location, income, ethnicity, disability and other categories.

Increased demands on the global statistical system
The need for improved monitoring poses enormous challenges to the global statistical system. Data sources and survey instruments currently employed in global and national monitoring cannot provide real-time data and finely disaggregated data. The capacity of many developing countries to monitor several MDG indicators is still weak and often dependent on the support or initiatives of international organizations. The post-2015 development agenda will put a lot of additional demands on the statistical systems of developing countries.

FAO's Voices of the Hungry project
The report of the High-level Panel recommends a food- and nutrition-specific sustainable development goal, with five targets. The first target calls for ending

(Cont.)

Food security and its four dimensions

■ Food availability: much improved, but progress is uneven across regions and over time

Food availability plays a prominent role in food security. Supplying enough food to a given population is a necessary, albeit not a sufficient, condition to ensure that people have adequate access to food. Over the last two decades, food supplies have grown faster than the population in developing countries, resulting in rising food availability per person. Dietary energy supplies have also risen faster than average dietary energy requirements, resulting in higher levels of energy adequacy in most developing regions, bar Western Asia (Table 2). Average dietary energy supply adequacy – dietary energy supply as a percentage of the average dietary energy requirement – has risen by almost 10 percent over the last two decades in developing regions as a whole. This improvement is consistent with the reduction in undernourishment from about 24 percent to 14 percent of total population between 1990–92 and 2011–13.

The quality of diets has also improved. This is reflected, for instance, in the decline in the share of dietary energy derived from cereals and roots and tubers in most regions since 1990–92 (Figure 8). Overall, the diets of developing regions have seen a number of improvements over the last two decades. For example, per capita availability of fruits

and vegetables, livestock products and vegetable oils increased by 90, 70 and 32 percent, respectively, since 1990–92. This has translated into generally improved diets, including a 20 percent increase in protein availability per person. Only Africa and Southern Asia did not benefit fully from these improvements; diets in these regions remain imbalanced and heavily dependent on cereals and roots and tubers.

Major contributions to food availability come not only from agriculture, but also from fisheries, aquaculture and forest products. It is estimated that between 15 and 20 percent of all animal protein consumed is derived from aquatic animals, which are highly nutritious and serve as a valuable supplement to diets lacking essential vitamins and minerals. Forests provide a wide range of highly nutritious foods, in the form of leaves, seeds, nuts, honey, fruits, mushrooms, insects and wild animals. In Burkina Faso, for example, tree foods constitute an important share of rural diets. It has been reported that 100 grams of a fruit from the baobab tree correspond to 100 percent of a child's recommended daily allowance of iron and potassium, 92 percent of the recommended daily allowance of copper and 40 percent of the recommended daily allowance of calcium. An estimated 2.4 billion people, or about one-third of the population in developing regions, depend on fuelwood for cooking, sterilizing water and preserving food.

TABLE 2

Average dietary energy supply adequacy in the developing regions, 1990–92 to 2011–13

	1990–92	2000–02	2005–07	2008–10	2011–13*
	(Percentage)				
World	114	117	119	120	122
Developed regions	131	134	136	135	135
Developing regions	108	112	114	117	118
Least-developed countries	97	97	101	103	105
Landlocked developing countries	99	98	104	107	110
Small island developing states	103	109	111	113	114
Low-income economies	97	96	101	102	105
Lower-middle-income economies	107	107	110	112	114
Low-income food-deficit countries	104	103	106	108	110
Africa	108	110	113	115	117
Northern Africa	138	139	139	141	144
Sub-Saharan Africa	100	103	108	109	111
Asia	107	111	113	116	117
Caucasus and Central Asia		105	118	120	125
Eastern Asia	107	118	119	124	124
South-Eastern Asia	99	106	112	116	121
Southern Asia	106	104	105	106	108
Western Asia	142	135	135	134	134
Latin America and the Caribbean	117	121	124	125	127
Caribbean	101	109	110	112	114
Latin America	118	122	124	126	128
Oceania	113	112	115	116	116

Note: * Projections.
Source: FAO.

FIGURE **8**

The share of dietary energy supply derived from cereals, roots and tubers has declined in most regions since 1990–92, indicating improving dietary quality

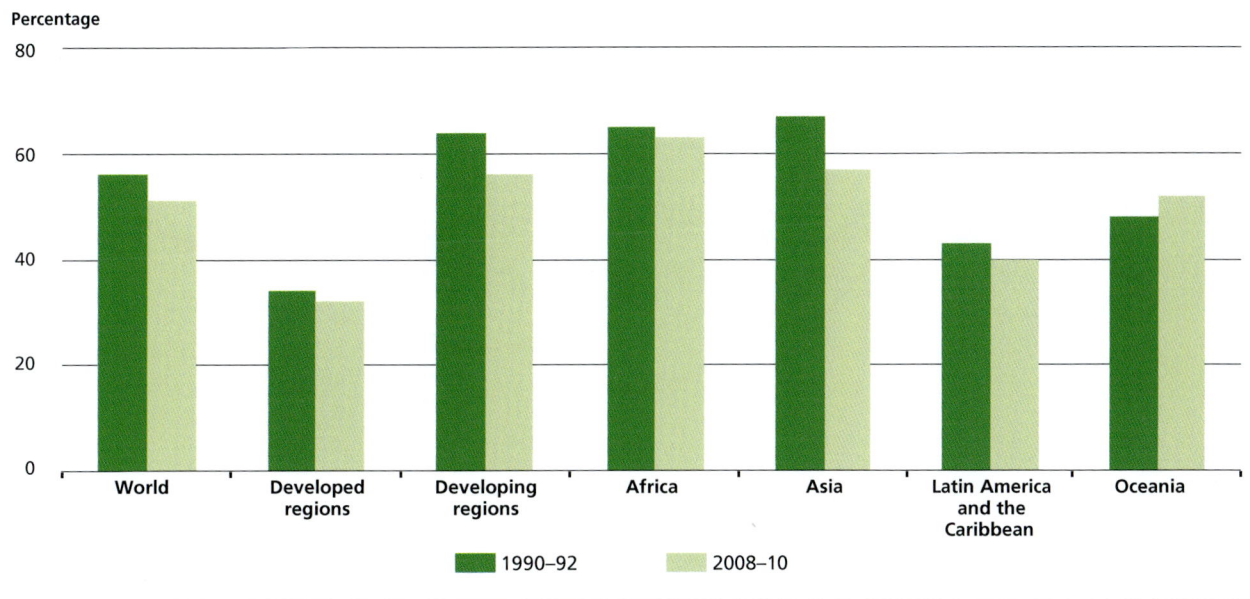

Source: FAO.

Access to food: significantly improved, in line with poverty reduction

The ability to access food rests on two pillars: economic and physical access. Economic access is determined by disposable income, food prices and the provision of and access to social support. Physical access is determined by the availability and quality of infrastructure, including ports, roads, railways, communication and food storage facilities and other installations that facilitate the functioning of markets. Incomes earned in agriculture, forests, fisheries and aquaculture play a primary role in determining food security outcomes.

Improvements in economic access to food can be reflected by reduction in poverty rates. Poverty and undernourishment have both declined over the past 20 years, albeit at different rates. Between 1990 and 2010 undernourishment rates declined from 24 percent to 15 percent in developing regions as a whole, while poverty rates fell from 47 percent to 24 percent in 2008 (Figure 9).

Economic access to food is also determined by food prices and people's purchasing power. The domestic food price index, defined as the ratio of food purchasing power parity (PPP) to general PPP, captures the cost of food relative to total consumption. The ratio has been on an increasing trend since 2001, but is now found to be at levels consistent with longer-term trends for most regions (Figure 10).

FIGURE **9**

MDG 1 target achievement trajectories and actual progress on key indicators, all developing regions

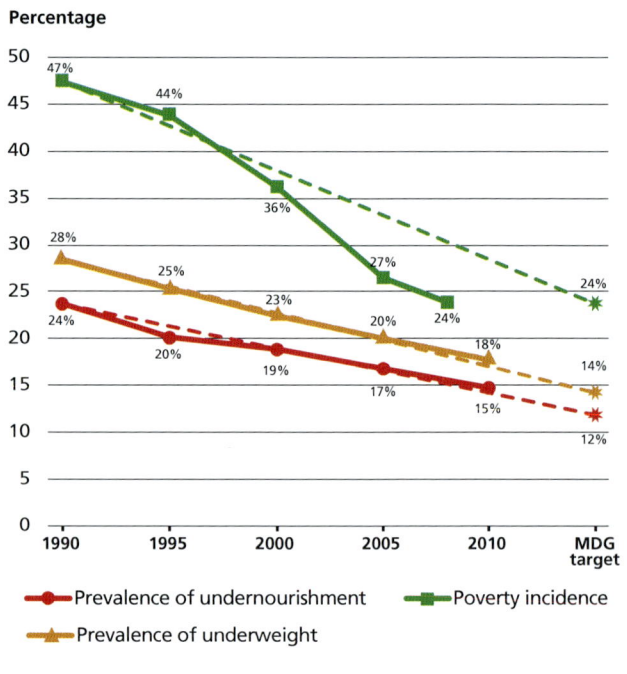

Source: FAO.

FIGURE **10**

Evolution of the domestic food price index in selected regions

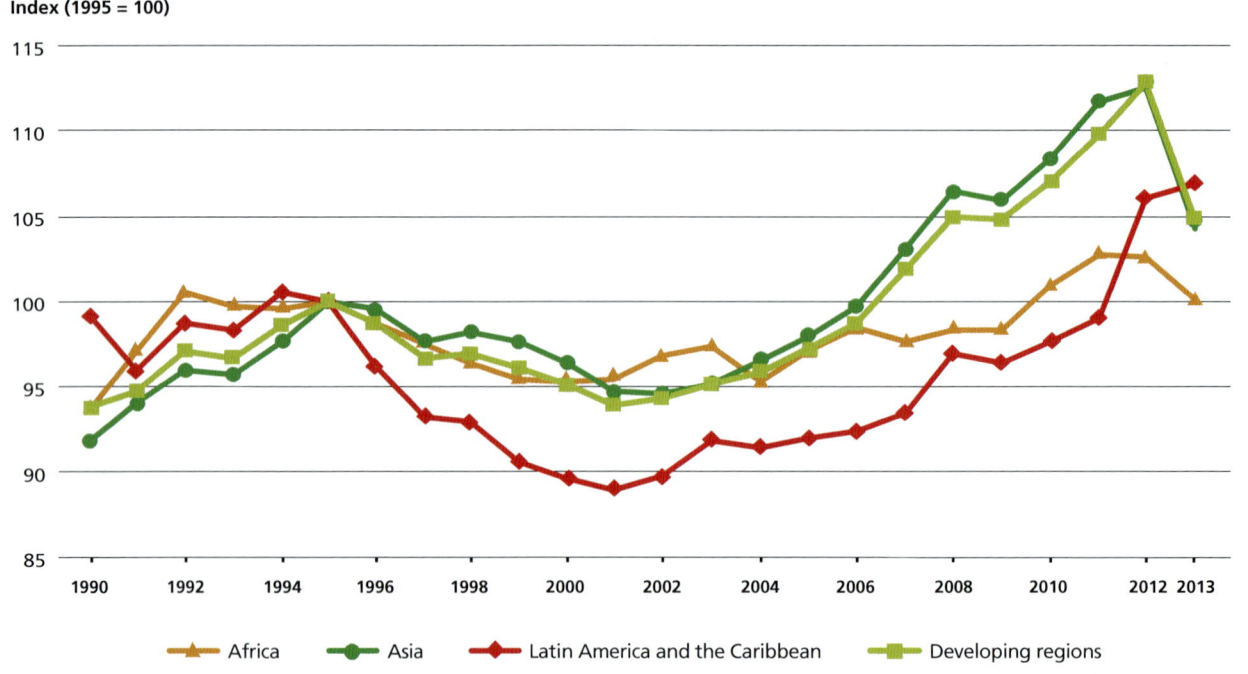

Source: FAO.

Food utilization: marked improvements are evident in both determinants and outcomes

Food utilization includes two distinct dimensions. The first is captured by anthropometric indicators affected by undernutrition that are widely available for children under five years of age. These include wasting (being too thin for one's height), stunting (being too short for one's age) and underweight (being too thin for one's age). Measurements of children under five years of age are considered effective approximations of the nutritional status of the entire population. The second dimension is captured by a number of determinants or input indicators that reflect food quality and preparations, health and hygiene conditions, determining how effectively available food can be utilized.

Outcome indicators of food utilization convey the impact of inadequate food intake and poor health. Wasting, for instance, is the result of short-term inadequacy of food intake, an illness or an infection, whereas stunting is often caused by prolonged inadequacy of food intake, repeated episodes of infections and/or repeated episodes of acute undernutrition.

Prevalence rates for stunting and underweight in children under five years of age have declined in all developing regions since 1990, indicating improved nutrition resulting from enhanced access to and availability of food (Figure 11). Figure 11 shows that progress in reducing the prevalence of stunting has been slightly more limited than for underweight for most regions. However, many countries in Africa still report prevalence rates of 30 percent or more, which the World Health Organization (WHO) classifies as high or very high.[3] The worst-affected countries are concentrated in Eastern Africa and the Sahel. A few countries in Southern Asia also report stunting rates of up to 50 percent.

Progress in terms of food access and availability is not always accompanied by progress in food utilization. This reflects, to some extent, the nature of malnutrition and its associated anthropometric indicators, which capture not only the effects of food insecurity but also those of poor health and diseases such as diarrhoea, malaria, HIV/AIDS and tuberculosis. Stunting, in particular, is a largely irreversible symptom of undernutrition; hence improvements will only be visible over a longer period of time.

Underweight is a much more sensitive and more direct indicator of food utilization, showing improvements more promptly than does stunting. But again, changes at the global level mask considerable differences among regions. Much of the reduction in the prevalence of underweight in children under the age of five can be attributed to improvements in Asian countries. While Asia as a region still exhibits the highest prevalence of underweight in preschool children, Asia also recorded the greatest improvement since 1990, with prevalence rates falling from 33 percent in 1990

to 20 percent in 2010. Progress has been much slower in Africa, where prevalence rates declined from 23 percent in 1990 to 18 percent in 2010 (Figure 11).

Food utilization is also influenced by the way in which food is handled, prepared and stored. Good health is a prerequisite for the human body to absorb nutrients effectively, and hygienic food helps maintain a healthy body. Access to clean water is crucial to preparation of clean, healthy food and maintaining a healthy body.

The last 20 years have seen significant progress in this area. By 2010, the share of the world's population without access to adequate drinking water has fallen to 12 percent from 24 percent in 1990; thus, the MDG target of halving the proportion of the population without sustainable access to safe drinking water and basic sanitation has already been reached at the global level. Again, however, progress has been uneven across regions and limited in sub-Saharan Africa (Figure 12). The most recent data available suggest that only 61 percent of the population in sub-Saharan Africa has access to improved water supply, compared with 90 percent in Northern Africa, Latin America and most of Asia. Similar disparities are found within countries and, in particular, between urban and rural areas.

FIGURE 11

Prevalence of stunting and underweight in children under five years of age, by region

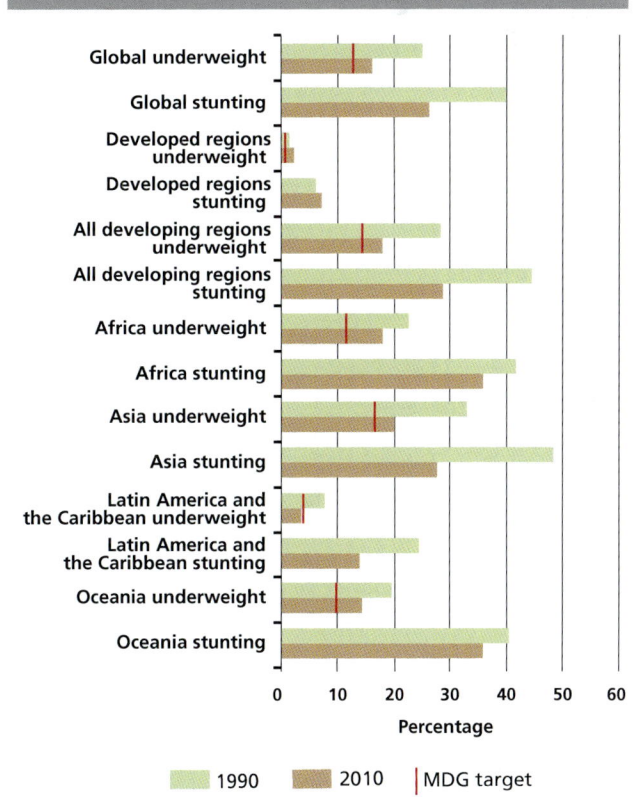

Source: WHO-UNICEF Joint Global Nutrition Database, 2011 revision (completed July 2012).

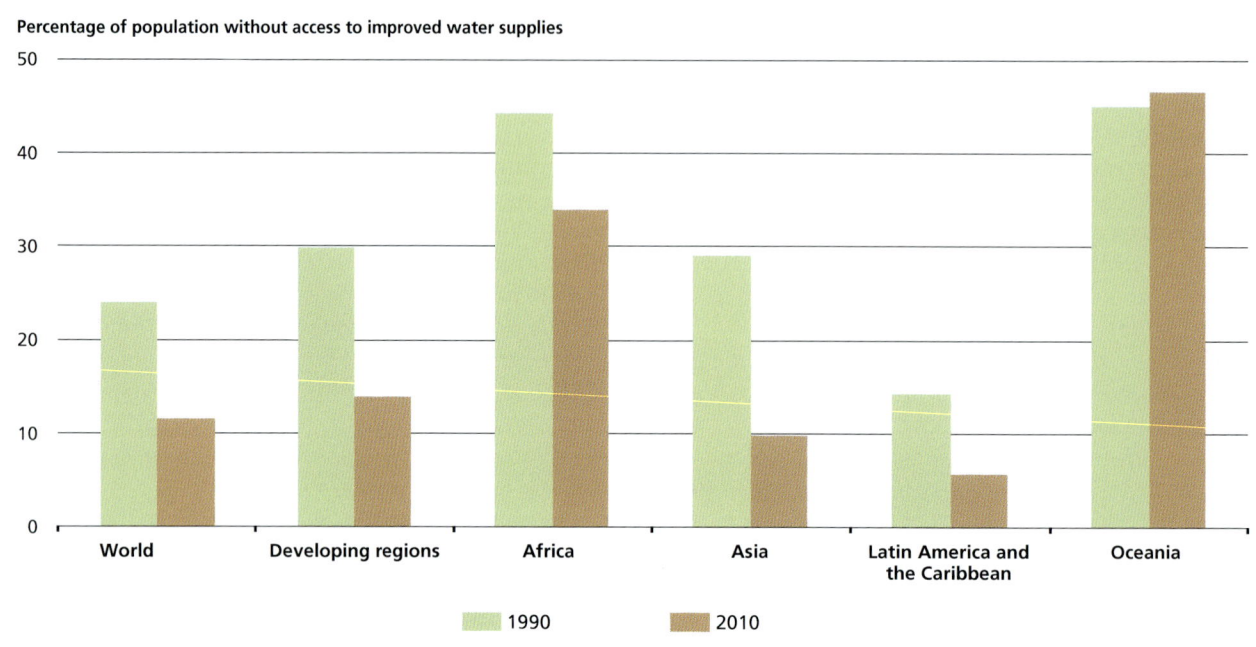

FIGURE 12

Vast progress has been made in providing access to safe water supplies

Percentage of population without access to improved water supplies

1990   2010

Source: FAO.

▪ Stability: exposure to short-term risks may endanger long-term progress

Two types of indicator have been identified to measure the extent and exposure to risk. Key indicators for exposure to risk include the area equipped for irrigation, which provides a measure of the extent of exposure to climatic shocks such as droughts, and the share of food imports in total merchandise exports, which captures the adequacy of foreign exchange reserves to pay for food imports. A second group of indicators captures risks or shocks that directly affect food security, such as swings in food and input prices, production and supply. The suite of indicators covers a number of stability measures, including an indicator of political instability available from the World Bank.

A thorough and comprehensive review of stability measures is not possible here because of space constraints. The content that follows takes a limited and more focused look at two important aspects of stability, namely those that pertain to food supply and food price stability.

The recent vagaries of international food markets have moved vulnerability to food insecurity to the forefront of the food policy debate. However, newly available data on changes in consumer prices for food suggest that the changes in prices on international commodity markets may have had less impact on consumer prices than initially expected (see *What was the impact of price volatility observed over recent years?,* page 13). Where world price

shocks induced high domestic volatility, food producers risked losing the inputs and capital they had invested. The low capacity of small-scale producers, such as smallholder farmers, to cope with large swings in input and output prices makes them risk-averse, lowers their propensity to adopt and invest in new technologies and ultimately results in lower overall production.

Together with swings in prices, food supplies have seen larger-than-normal variability in recent years. However, there is also evidence that production variability is lower than price variability, and that consumption variability is smaller than both production and price variability. Among the main regions, Africa and Latin America and the Caribbean have experienced the widest fluctuation in food supply since 1990, while variability has been smaller in Asia. Variability in food production per capita was greatest in Africa and Latin America and the Caribbean (Figure 13).

The vulnerability dimension of food security is increasingly cast in the context of climate change. The number of extreme events such as droughts, floods and hurricanes has increased in recent years, as has the unpredictability of weather patterns, leading to substantial losses in production and lower incomes in vulnerable areas. Changeable weather patterns have played a part in increasing food price levels and variability. Smallholder farmers, pastoralists and poor consumers have been particularly badly affected by these sudden changes.

Climate change may play an even more prominent role in the coming decades. Mitigating its impacts and preserving

FIGURE 13

Food production has varied widely in developing regions since 1990, with marked regional differences

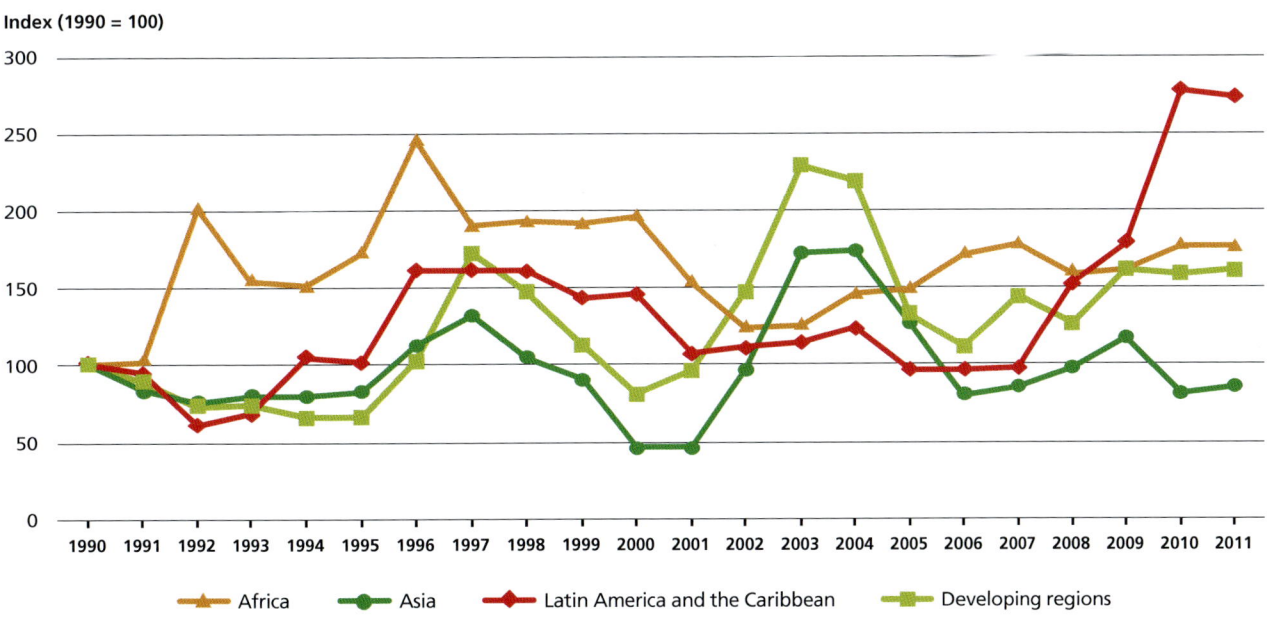

Index (1990 = 100)

Note: Food PIN variability in year t is calculated as the standard error deviation from the trend for the previous five years. It is a polynomial trend of order 3 over the period 1985 to 2011.
Source: FAO.

natural resources will be major objectives, especially in connection with the management of land, water, soil nutrients and genetic resources. Improved management of natural resources should focus on reducing variability in agricultural outputs and increasing resilience to shocks and long-term climate change.

The pressing need to improve natural resources management extends well beyond agriculture. Forests and trees outside forests play a large part in protecting soil and water resources. They promote soil fertility, regulate climate

and provide habitat for wild pollinators and the predators of agricultural pests. They can help stabilize agricultural output and provide protection from extreme weather events. According to FAO's *Global Forest Resources Assessment 2010*,[4] 8 percent of the world's forests (330 million hectares) are managed specifically to address soil and water conservation objectives. They not only provide a wide range of nutritious foods on a regular basis, but they also help protect access to food in the form of dietary supplements during times of poor yields, natural calamities and economic hardships.

Highlighting links in the suite of indicators

The next section, *Food security dimensions at the national level*, pages 29–41, dives deeper into the relationship between various food security indicators. A starting point is the matrix of correlations between indicators (Figure 14).[5] This is followed by an analysis at country level of the main associations and divergences between indicators. For instance, high rates of food availability occurring together with low rates of utilization would raise the question of

what impedes the effective use of available food. Likewise, high rates of undernourishment in the presence of low rates of poverty would raise the question of why the poor fail to get access to food. Divergences can also expose possible measurement problems. Whatever the case, deviations help shape a research agenda into the causes and consequences of food insecurity or related measurement issues.

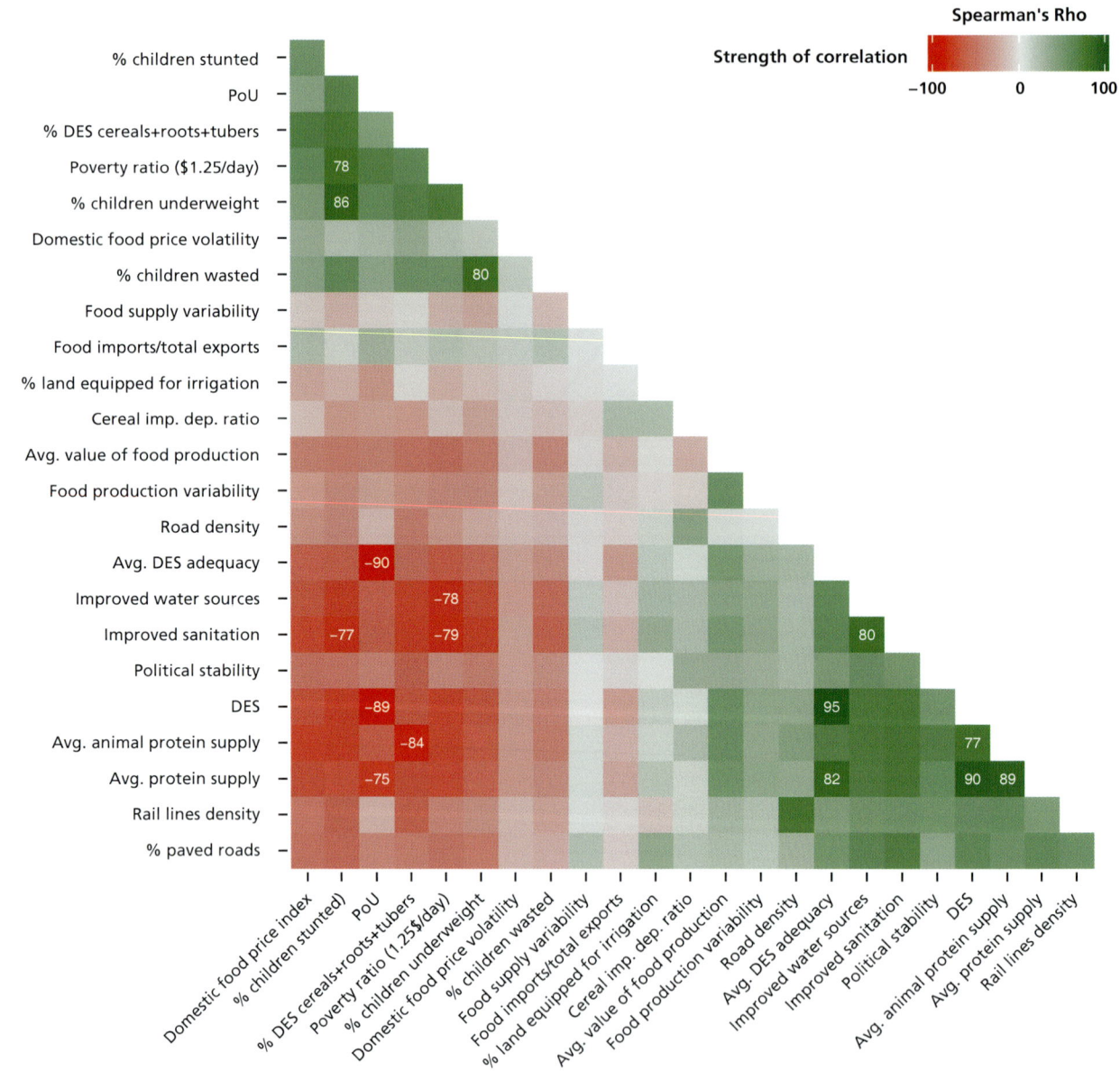

FIGURE 14

Correlation matrix of key food security indicators, all developing regions

Note: Complete descriptive titles for all food security indicators are shown in Figure 7 on page 16.
Source: FAO.

All the scatter plots in this section highlight six countries – Bangladesh, Ghana, Nepal, Nicaragua, Tajikistan and Uganda – that are described in the detailed case studies in the next section (*Food security dimensions at the national level,* pages 29–41). These countries were selected for a number of reasons, including the fact that they often show deviations from typical associations between two food security indicators.

■ **Q1: Does improved access to food also mean better utilization?**

In many countries this is the case. A low level of dietary energy intake, as shown by a high prevalence of undernourishment, commonly corresponds to high rates of other forms of malnutrition. A reduction in undernourishment is generally associated with improvements in the overall nutritional status of the population (Figure 15), although the association is rather weak, with an R^2 of only 28 percent.

The low R^2 reflects the frequent exceptions to the low-undernourishment/low-stunting rule, with many outlier countries in Northern Africa, Southern Asia and sub-Saharan Africa. One such outlier in sub-Saharan Africa is Ghana, where the prevalence of undernourishment was less than 5 percent in 2011–13, but more than 29 percent of children under five years of age were reported to be stunted. A similar picture emerges for Nepal. Mali is an extreme case: prevalence of undernourishment was estimated at 7 percent in 2011–13, while 38 percent of children under five years of age were stunted. The same is true for Viet Nam, with a prevalence of undernourishment of 8 percent in 2011–13, but more than 32 percent of children under five years old were stunted.

Instances of relatively low undernourishment but high malnutrition may call for policy measures and related programmes aimed at improving access to safe and nutritious food, promoting dietary diversity, improving food safety and supporting hygiene. Stunting, in particular, could be the outcome of repeated episodes of wasting, which may have occurred recently enough for the impacts to still be visible, despite an overall improvement in food security. Such conditions may arise in countries in which undernourishment has declined significantly in a short period of time.

FIGURE 15

The relationship between the prevalence of undernourishment and the percentage of preschool children who are stunted is quite weak

Prevalence of undernourishment

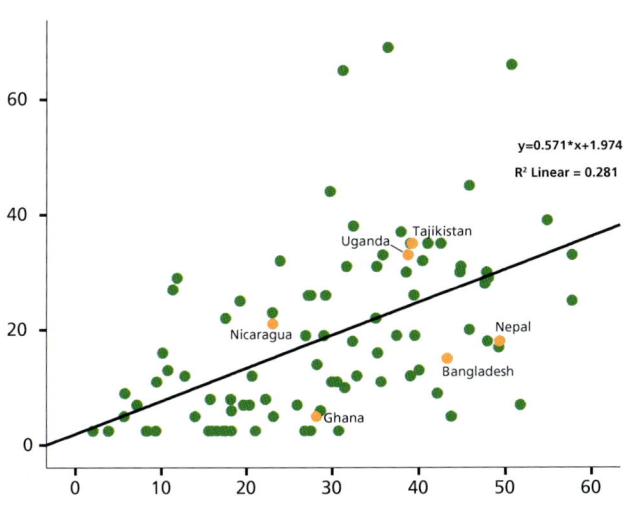

$y=0.571*x+1.974$
R^2 Linear = 0.281

Percentage of children under five years of age who are stunted

Source: FAO and WHO.

FIGURE 16

The adequacy of food supply and prevalence of undernourishment are strongly linked

Prevalence of undernourishment

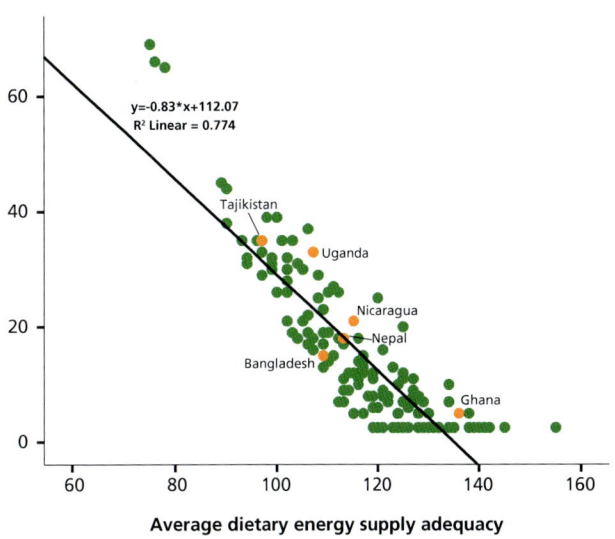

$y=-0.83*x+112.07$
R^2 Linear = 0.774

Average dietary energy supply adequacy

Source: FAO.

■ Q2: Does high food availability imply lower undernourishment?

By and large, countries in which food supplies generally exceed the amount of food required by the population also show low levels of undernourishment and undernutrition. This is evident, for instance, when the prevalence of undernourishment is plotted against the adequacy of average dietary energy supply (Figure 16), and confirmed in the detailed country analyses presented in the next section.

The association between food availability, as measured by adequacy of average dietary energy supply, and the prevalence of undernourishment is partly related to the construction of the indicators. The adequacy of average dietary energy supply expresses the dietary energy supply as a percentage of the average dietary energy requirement, and thus this indicator captures elements applied in measuring undernourishment. The remaining divergences reflect differences in access (distributional measures in the prevalence of undernourishment indicator) and the fact that the prevalence of undernourishment is based on minimum dietary energy requirements.

■ Q3: Does high food availability imply better food utilization?

In many countries a similar association holds when indicators related to the utilization of food, such as the percentage of children under the age of five who are stunted, are compared with food availability indicators, such as adequacy of dietary energy supply (Figure 17). This is the case in most countries discussed in next section, especially in Bangladesh, Ghana and Nepal. But it also holds for several other African countries, including Benin, Guinea-Bissau, Mali and the Niger, all of which have stunting rates of up to 50 percent. In these cases, abundant food supplies have not translated into better utilization of food and improved nutrition. This suggests that policy interventions that improve these aspects of food security may render high returns. Depending on local context, such measures could include policies aimed at improving nutrition, support to increased dietary diversity and food supplementation programmes.

Country-level results suggest that poor dietary quality is often associated with poor utilization outcomes, in particular with high stunting rates (Figure 18). This finding is confirmed by the more in-depth analysis presented in the country case studies which appear later in this report. The exception is Uganda, where diets are traditionally diverse and energy is derived from foods other than cereals, roots and tubers, such as *matooke*, a type of banana.

Other exceptions include Burundi and Pakistan, where calories from staples account for less than 50 percent of dietary energy supply, yet the prevalence of stunting is high: 58 percent in Burundi, and 43 percent in Pakistan. In Pakistan, balanced diets are not available to the poorer segments of the population, which rely heavily on a few carbohydrate-rich staples. Policies may therefore be needed to further support safety nets and access to more diverse and nutritious food for the poor. Investments in education and health services are also needed. Best practices for breastfeeding and the provision of fortified foods may also be important. In Burundi, however, the overall amount of food available is low, and even an equally distributed food supply may not help avoid adverse anthropometric outcomes, such as a high prevalence of stunting. In this context, policies to consider include prioritizing increases in food supplies through increased production and, possibly, imports.

■ Q4: Does poverty reduction always imply hunger reduction?

Poverty plays an important role in the access dimension of food security. Extreme poverty, as measured by the proportion of people living on $1.25 a day or less, has declined considerably since 1990, albeit unevenly across regions and countries.[6] In 1990, the share of people living in absolute poverty was as high as 48 percent in the developing regions. Declines were greatest in China and other East Asian countries but much less in sub-Saharan Africa and Southern Asia. Overall, preliminary estimates suggest that the developing world reached the MDG target of halving the proportion of people living in extreme poverty in 2008, with 24 percent of people living on $1.25 a day or less.

FIGURE **17**

The relationship between adequacy of food supply and stunting is weak

Percentage of children under five years of age who are stunted

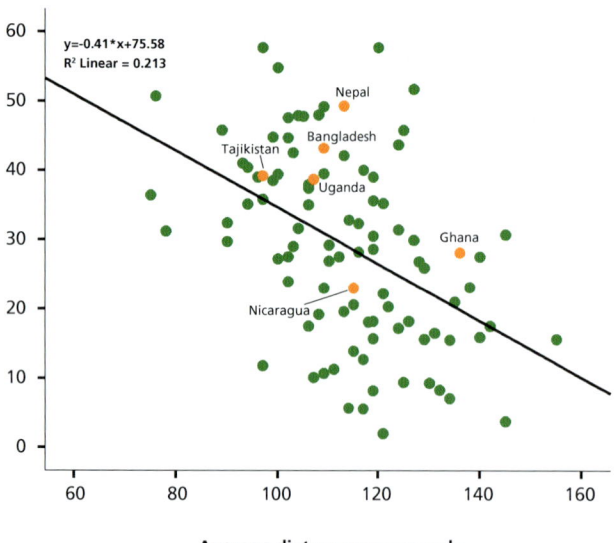

Average dietary energy supply

Source: FAO and WHO.

FIGURE **18**

An increase in proportion of starchy foods in the diet can lead to increased stunting

Percentage of children under five years of age who are stunted

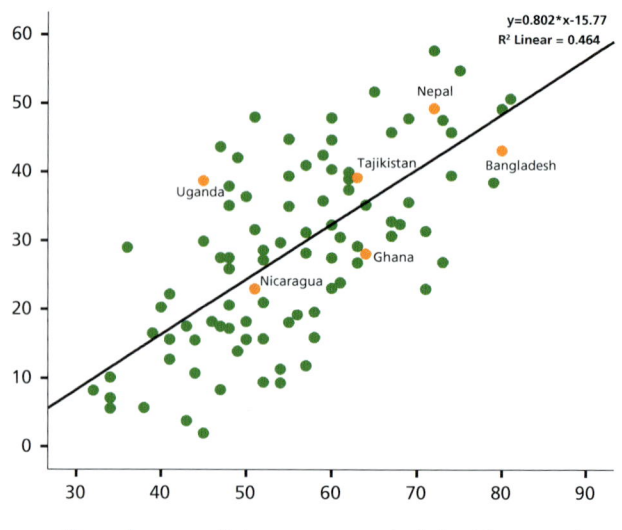

Share of average dietary energy supply derived from cereals, roots and tubers

Source: FAO and WHO.

Higher levels of poverty are linked with higher prevalence of undernourishment (Figure 19), although there is not a one-to-one correlation between hunger and extreme poverty. Low levels of extreme poverty, for instance, do not necessarily mean low levels of undernourishment, as seen in the case of Tajikistan. The country is characterized by a low level of agricultural productivity and, at the same time, food appears to play a prominent role among essential goods for large shares of the population. In such circumstances, enhancing productivity, the effectiveness of food distribution systems and their ability to deliver enough safe and nutritious food that consumers can access may result in quick wins in the fight against both poverty and hunger.

In other countries, high levels of extreme poverty are associated with low levels of food utilization as a result of factors such as lack of access to safe water and sanitation. Examples include Bangladesh and Ghana among the countries discussed in the next section, along with, for instance, Chad, Haiti, Liberia and Mozambique. In countries in which the prevalence of undernourishment is relatively low, large percentages of the population are approaching an income level at which their demand for food safety and hygiene starts rising faster than their demand for additional basic calories.

There are also countries showing high levels of extreme poverty and relatively low levels of undernourishment: these include, *inter alia*, Nepal, Swaziland and Viet Nam. This combination tends to be more common than that in which food insecurity is higher than poverty. In these countries, the root causes of poverty are less directly related to food production and distribution systems, and more likely linked to other economic activities. Therefore, poverty reduction strategies may need to focus on entry points other than food and agriculture.

Where food insecurity is more pervasive, its association with poverty becomes weaker. The reasons for this are varied. Relatively better-off consumers may, for instance, use some of their additional income to purchase non-food items such as cellular phones (an increasingly essential communication tool), or to shift to more expensive foods, for example from cassava to rice or from cereals to livestock products. Some of these shifts may do nothing to increase energy intake or improve nutrition.

Finally, a close inspection of the available country data also points to possible measurement problems. For example, in Nicaragua in 2005, the proportion of people

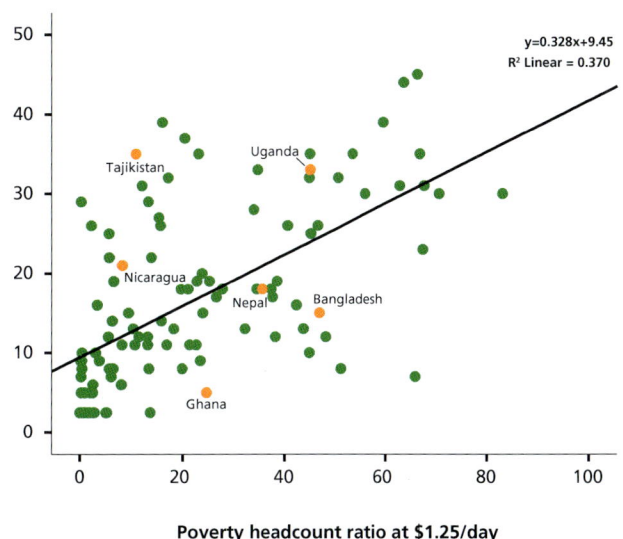

FIGURE **19**

Undernourishment and poverty rates generally correlate at the country level, albeit with some exceptions

Prevalence of undernourishment

y=0.328x+9.45
R² Linear = 0.370

Poverty headcount ratio at $1.25/day

Source: FAO and World Bank.

living in extreme poverty was estimated at 12 percent, while 25.5 percent of the people were chronically undernourished in 2005–07. There is evidence that this disparity reflects a peculiarity in the distribution of people around the extreme poverty threshold – $1.25 a day – and their energy intake. For many people, small amounts of money may help them escape extreme poverty, but not hunger. For example, in Nicaragua in 2005, those in extreme poverty lived on just over 9 córdobas a day, the equivalent of $1.25, which on average bought only 1 459 kcal, as compared with FAO's minimum dietary energy requirement of 1 819 kcal per day. But many people find themselves just over the extreme poverty threshold: about 32 percent of the population of Nicaragua lived on 14.6 córdobas ($2) or less in 2005. Thus, about 20 percent of the population were between the extreme poverty and the poverty thresholds. On average, in 2005 14.6 córdobas could buy 1 792 kcal, still less than the minimum amount needed for light activity and minimum acceptable weight.

Key messages

- Food security is a complex condition. Its dimensions – availability, access, utilization and stability – are better understood when presented through a suite of indicators.

- Over the last 20 years, food availability in developing regions has risen faster than the average dietary energy requirements, while the quality of diets has improved. Better economic access to food is reflected by changes in poverty rates, which have fallen along with undernourishment over this period, albeit at different speeds. The recent vagaries of international food markets have moved vulnerability to the forefront of discussions of food insecurity. The impact of price variability and spikes on consumers may have been more limited than initially expected, while food producers faced high risks.

- Hunger tends to be widespread in countries with high poverty levels. Hunger is likely to be more severe than poverty, especially when both are at elevated levels. As food is one of the most income-responsive of all basic necessities, boosting incomes and providing social safety nets reduce hunger. Where undernourishment is less prevalent than poverty, interventions to improve food utilization are required.

- Ample food availability does not necessarily enable better food access and utilization. When poor access and utilization occur, despite sufficient food availability, social protection, as well as improvements in food distribution and supplementation programmes, should be prioritized.

- Undernourishment and undernutrition can coexist. However, in some countries, undernutrition rates, as indicated by the proportion of stunted children, are considerably higher than the prevalence of undernourishment, as indicated by inadequacy of dietary energy supply. In these countries, nutrition-enhancing interventions are crucial to improve the nutritional aspects of food security. Improvements require a range of food security and nutrition-enhancing interventions in agriculture, health, hygiene, water supply and education, particularly targeting women.

Food security dimensions at the national level

Although the 2015 MDG hunger goal remains within reach, progress is not even and many countries are unlikely to meet the goal of halving the prevalence of undernourishment by 2015. Many of these countries face severe constraints. For example, countries that have experienced conflict during the past two decades are more likely to have seen significant setbacks in reducing hunger. Landlocked countries often lag behind coastal countries as they face persistent challenges in accessing world markets, while developing countries with poor infrastructure and weak institutions find it difficult to implement policies to increase agricultural productivity and address inequities of access to food.

This section looks at six countries – Bangladesh, Ghana, Nepal, Nicaragua, Tajikistan and Uganda – in more detail, finding a mixed picture of progress and setbacks, successes and shortfalls in the fight against hunger. Reducing poverty and hunger requires successful efforts over a long period of time, but the conditions – environmental, social, economic and political – that leave people vulnerable vary considerably from one country to another.

Bangladesh, Ghana and Nicaragua have all managed to halve the prevalence of undernourishment since the beginning of the 1990s. This achievement is the result of a combination of factors, such as robust economic growth over decades, freer trade and, for Ghana and Nicaragua, political stability and favourable international market conditions characterized by high export prices. But, above all, it was the commitment of consecutive governments to long-term rural development and poverty-reducing plans that has shaped the dynamics of change.

Nepal experienced a period of prolonged conflict and political uncertainty which weakened the effectiveness of its institutions in both producing food and improving access to it. Nevertheless, the country seems on track to reach the MDG hunger goal by 2015. Tajikistan, landlocked and with poor infrastructure and little additional land to bring into agricultural production, looks unlikely to reach the hunger target. Incomplete land reform in Tajikistan has slowed growth in agricultural productivity and incomes, but this has to some extent been offset by inflow of remittances from migrants.

Uganda still faces significant challenges in under-nourishment. With one of the highest population growth rates in the world, low agricultural productivity growth and a large part of the population living on $1.25 a day or less, the country seems unlikely to reach the 2015 hunger target.

Bangladesh: Long-term commitment to food security spurs significant progress

Food security in Bangladesh is challenged by a host of factors ranging from the country's ever-increasing population density, climate change, scarce natural resources (with nearly no agricultural land left untilled), vulnerability to price shocks and persistent poverty. In spite of these constraints, Bangladesh has already met the MDG hunger target (Figure 20). This remarkable feat was achieved in the context of rapid economic growth in the 1990s spurred by significant growth in agricultural productivity[7] and driven by a combination of factors including macroeconomic stability, liberalization of input markets and opening up of the economy.

FIGURE **20**

Bangladesh has already met its MDG hunger target, dietary energy supply is adequate and stable and food production continues to increase

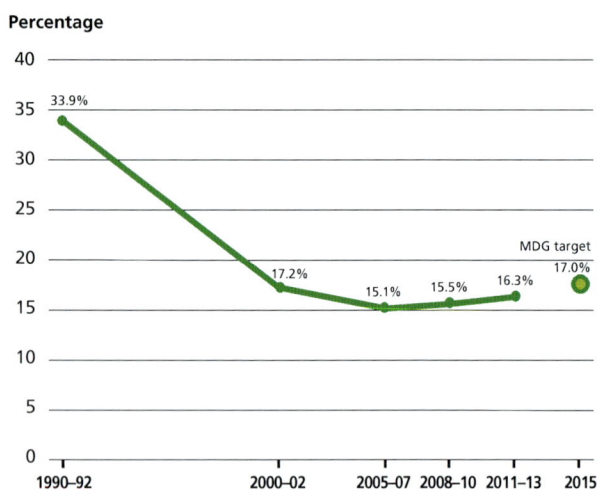

Prevalence of undernourishment

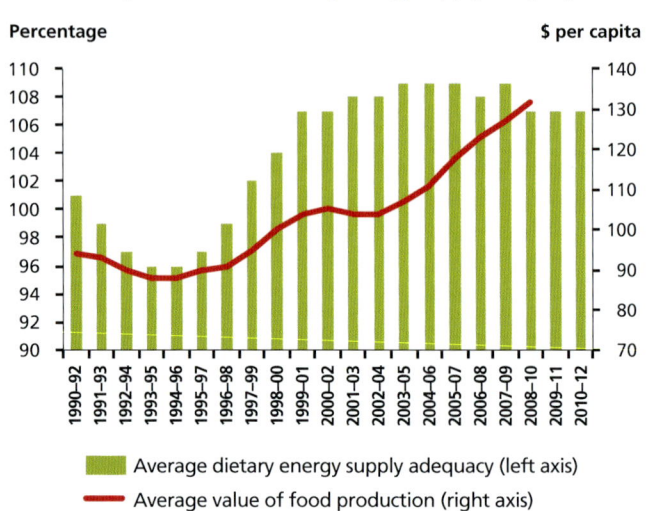

Food production and dietary energy supply adequacy

Note: Average value of food production denominated in 2004–06 international prices.
Source: FAO.

However, some 25 million people remain undernourished, and the prevalence of undernourishment has been rising slowly since the mid-2000s. Food security therefore remains high on the agenda of the government, and is being mainstreamed in policies. A comprehensive National Food Policy developed in 2008 was followed in 2011 by the Country Investment Plan, which provides stakeholders with a clear roadmap for investment in agriculture, food security and nutrition.

Agricultural productivity has increased substantially, with average yields and the value of food production per capita rising significantly since the mid-1990s (Figure 20). Private seed firms are being encouraged to enter the agricultural seed sector and regulatory frameworks are being strengthened.[8] Irrigation has spread widely through sustained public infrastructure development programmes, but the focus has now shifted to promoting water-saving farming practices to deal with declining aquifer levels and the increasing cost of irrigation.[9] Bangladesh Bank is increasing credit supply to farmers in an attempt to boost agricultural production; special attention is given to the needs of small-scale farmers because the vast and vibrant microfinance sector is unable to reach the poorest sections.[10]

The commitment of successive governments to poverty alleviation has resulted in considerable progress in poverty reduction, which mirrors growth in GDP per capita (Figure 21). The decline in poverty has been matched by similar declines in undernutrition, and Bangladesh appears to be on track to achieve its MDG target of reducing the percentage of children who are underweight to 33 percent by 2015 (Figure 21). However, considerable regional

disparities exist and progress in tackling undernutrition has been slowing in recent years. This indicates that higher incomes alone are not sufficient to reduce undernutrition. In 2009, cereals still provided 78.3 percent of all calories consumed. Moving away from cereals and into a variety of high-value food products would not only make more nutritious food available, but would also create an opportunity to increase farmers' incomes. The Country Investment Plan therefore gives priority to developing sustainable and diversified agriculture. The development of biofortified crops through programmes such as HarvestPlus and the Golden Rice Project is an example of how nutrition and agriculture can be integrated to tackle these issues.

Little progress has been made in reducing the proportion of women who are anaemic (42 percent in 2011 compared with 45 percent in 2004), and anaemia still constitutes a severe public health problem in the country. Gender-based differences, notably in wages and in access to inputs and markets, also have an impact on food security and nutrition.[11] Many households have chosen international and national migration as a livelihood strategy. From the early 1990s onwards, almost a quarter of a million people migrated abroad every year, generating an income inflow from remittances amounting to some 10 percent of GDP in 2011–12.[12]

Bangladesh has in place a significant safety net programme complemented by efforts of numerous non-governmental organizations (NGOs) to help those who are unable to reap the benefits from emerging productive

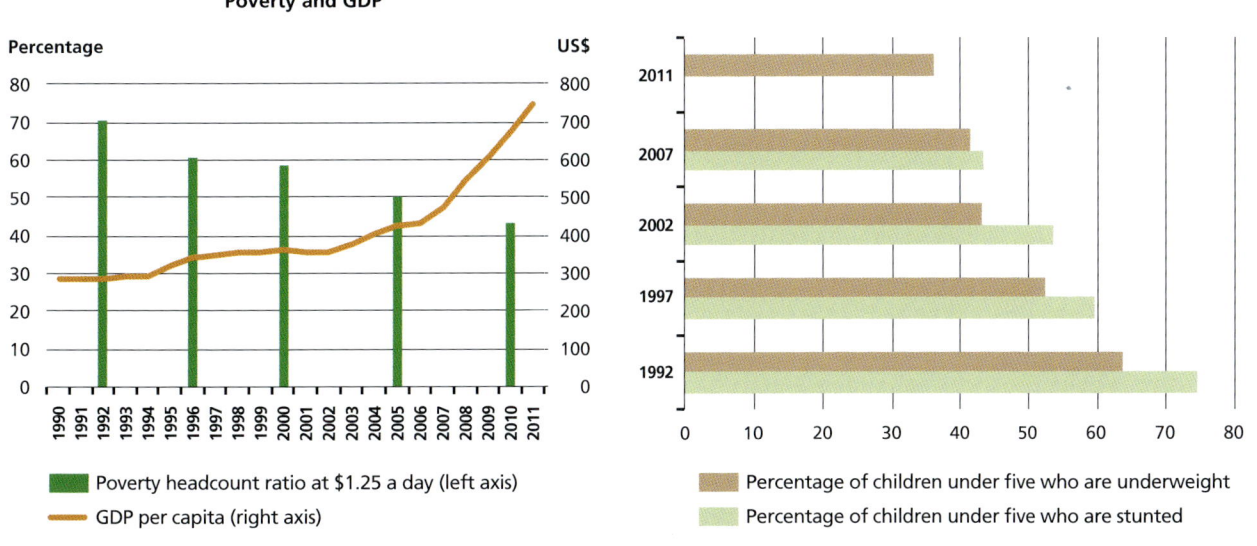

FIGURE 21

Bangladesh appears to be on track to meet its MDG targets for both poverty reduction and proportion of children who are stunted and underweight

Poverty and GDP

- Poverty headcount ratio at $1.25 a day (left axis)
- GDP per capita (right axis)

- Percentage of children under five who are underweight
- Percentage of children under five who are stunted

Note: Poverty threshold denominated in 2005 international prices.
Sources: World Development Indicators, 2012 (left); WHO, and National Institute of Population Research and Training (Bangladesh), *Bangladesh Demographic and Health Survey 2011* (right).

opportunities and the decline in poverty. This programme has been quite responsive to the adverse effects of price volatility on the poor. In reaction to the 2007–08 price crisis, for example, an employment generation programme was designed to provide financial relief to the most vulnerable during the lean seasons while building infrastructure. An improved version of this programme, together with other safety nets and NGO programmes, such as the multidonor Chars Livelihoods Programme, has succeeded in recent years in eradicating the often acute seasonal hunger experienced in the northwest of the country.

Problems of mistargeting and inefficiencies do exist, however, leaving some households outside of safety net assistance.[13] To deal with such issues, the government is developing a national social protection strategy, building on the success of existing programmes and including innovations meant to help the poor to graduate out of poverty.[14] The Country Investment Plan also aims to develop institutions and capacity to enhance the effectiveness of safety nets, calling for strengthening of partnerships with NGOs, some of which are experimenting with models that facilitate the graduation of households out of poverty.

Ghana: Impressive and broadly shared economic growth fuels food security achievement

Ghana is considered a success story in Africa for its robust economic growth over the past three decades – GDP grew by an average of 4.5 percent a year since 1983 and by an impressive 14 percent in 2011[15] (Figure 22). This has been fostered by political stability (Figure 23), market reforms, favourable terms of trade (higher gold and cocoa prices) and a good investment climate. The success of the

economic programmes and reforms show what sustained political commitment and partnership with the donor community can achieve.[16] Ghana is well on track to meet its MDG poverty target before 2015, and had met its 2015 MDG hunger target by 2000–02 (Figure 23). In 2011–13 less than 5 percent of the population were undernourished.

Ghana's economy depends heavily on agriculture; more than half of the country's workforce is involved in this sector. In the 1990s, a series of policies and institutional reforms, together with a corresponding set of investments, led to sustained increases in food production by Ghana's smallholder farmers.[17] Per capita food production increased by 55 percent between 1990–92 and 2008–10. Reforming the cocoa sector, which was implicitly taxed, played a crucial role in agricultural growth. Investments in research and development on roots and tubers and extension efforts were also successful in introducing innovative production methods, leading to yield increases and the development of new, more resilient varieties.[18]

Ghana's impressive GDP growth, averaging 5 percent per year since 2001, has reached a large part of the population, with extreme poverty declining from 51.7 percent in 1991 to 28.5 percent in 2006 (Figure 22). About 5 million people have been lifted out of poverty in just 15 years because the benefits of the rapid economic growth were broadly shared, especially with people in rural areas, who benefited from increased production and the creation of vibrant markets. The major beneficiaries of rising rural incomes were small-scale producers of cocoa and farmers producing fruits and vegetables.

Despite rapid progress in reducing poverty and hunger, Ghana has made less progress in reducing undernutrition (Figure 22). Although the proportion of children under five years of age who are underweight has been nearly halved since 1993–95, less progress has been made in reducing

prevalence of stunting, and about 23 percent of children under five years of age were stunted in 2011. Underlying causes of undernutrition include poverty, high disease burden and lack of access to deworming medication, lack of adequate child feeding practices at key stages of development and poor sanitation facilities. Inadequate access to sanitation facilities is a major cause of waterborne chronic diseases, acute infections and infant or child mortality. Despite considerable improvement in access to safe water sources over the past three decades, access to adequate sanitation facilities is still very poor.

Considerable differences still exist in poverty and nutrition at the regional level. Overall, rural people are up to four times more likely to live below the poverty line than are people in urban areas. The prevalence of poverty is the highest in the Northern, Upper East and Upper West regions, which are characterized agro-ecologically as rural savannah.[19]

These disparities are reflected in diets. People from worse-off areas consume a diet that is much less diverse and contains much less protein in the form of meat, fish, eggs or milk than do people in better-off areas.

The National Social Protection Strategy launched in 2007 is an integrated social protection framework that addresses the needs of vulnerable groups that have not benefited from economic growth. It targets policies to the extreme poor and highly vulnerable, notably through its main programme, Livelihood Empowerment Against Poverty, a conditional cash transfer programme.[20]

FIGURE 22

Ghana's GDP has increased rapidly and poverty has declined, but less progress has been made in reducing undernutrition

Poverty and GDP

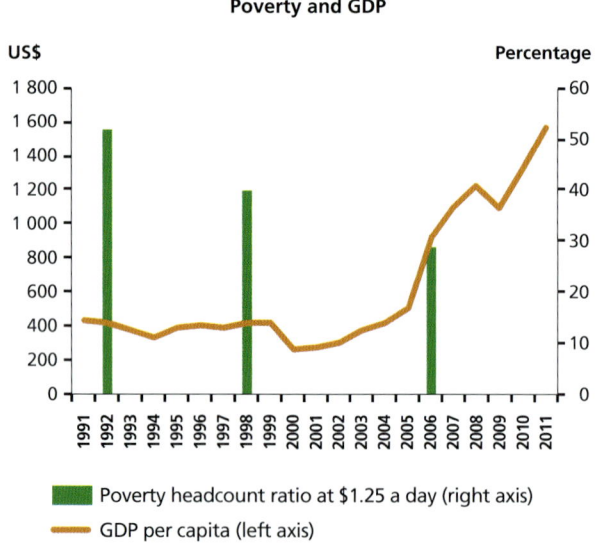

Poverty headcount ratio at $1.25 a day (right axis)
GDP per capita (left axis)

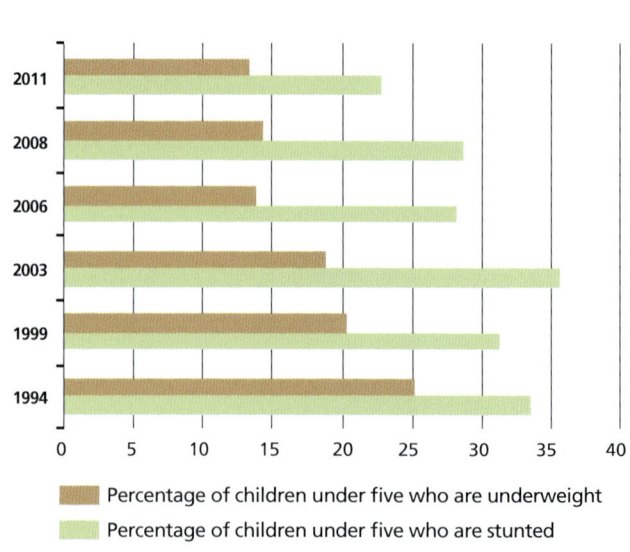

Percentage of children under five who are underweight
Percentage of children under five who are stunted

Note: Poverty threshold denominated in 2005 international prices.
Sources: World Development Indicators, 2012 (left); WHO, and Ministry of Health (Ghana), 2013, *National Multiple Indicator Cluster Survey, 2011* (right).

FIGURE 23

Peace and political stability contributed to Ghana achieving its 2015 MDG hunger target by 2000–02

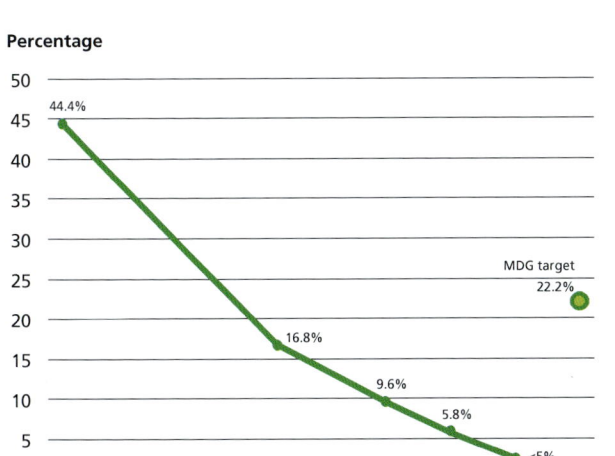

Prevalence of undernourishment

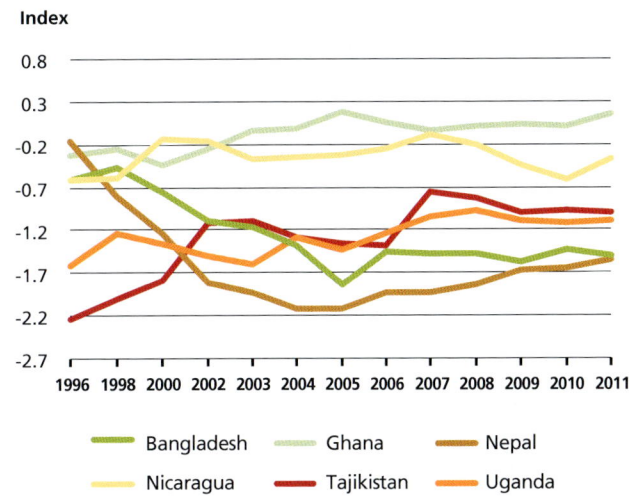

Index of political stability and absence of violence

Note: For the definition of political stability and absence of violence, see the Food Security Indicators available at http://www.fao.org/economic/ess/ess-fs/fs-data/en/.
Sources: FAO (left) and Brookings Institution, World Bank Development Research Group and World Bank Institute (right).

Nepal: Political stability is necessary to make progress sustainable and more evenly distributed

Nepal has made great strides in its fight against hunger since 1990–92, with the prevalence of undernourishment declining from 25.4 percent in 1990–92 to 16.0 percent in 2011–13. If it continues to progress at this rate, it will reach the MDG target on hunger by 2015 (Figure 24). This progress is all the more remarkable given the civil strife from the mid-1990s to 2006, the weakness of the country's infrastructure and the relatively low state of development of agriculture. In spite of progress in the fight against hunger, however, undernutrition is still widespread. The prevalences of underweight and stunting in children are among the highest in the world. Between 1995 and 2011, the prevalence of underweight in children declined from 44 to 29 percent, while the prevalence of stunting declined from 64 to 40 percent (Figure 24). Combating undernutrition poses great challenges for both short-term (e.g. implementation of safety nets) and long-term (e.g. structural development) policy measures.

Nepal is a predominantly mountainous country with poor transport, communication and power infrastructure. Agriculture, the mainstay of its economy, is hindered by relatively low productivity as compared with other countries in the region, and by a limited land resource base. Lack of roads, inadequate capital, insufficient access to output and input markets and poor access to affordable credit hinder the adoption of modern and productive farming technologies, resulting in producers relying on traditional agriculture.

Although policies have been in place to promote agricultural research, technology adoption and infrastructure development, their impact was diluted by both the years of conflict and the prolonged political transition that followed (see Figure 23), both of which resulted in a decline in the effectiveness of some institutions and programmes. Nevertheless, the average dietary energy supply in the country has been adequate to meet the food requirements of the population (Figure 25), partly as a result of modest increases in food production since 1990–92 (the value of food production per capita has increased by 12 percent) and partly because of increased food imports.

FIGURE 24

Nepal has made good progress in its fight against hunger, and is on track to meet the MDG hunger target by 2015

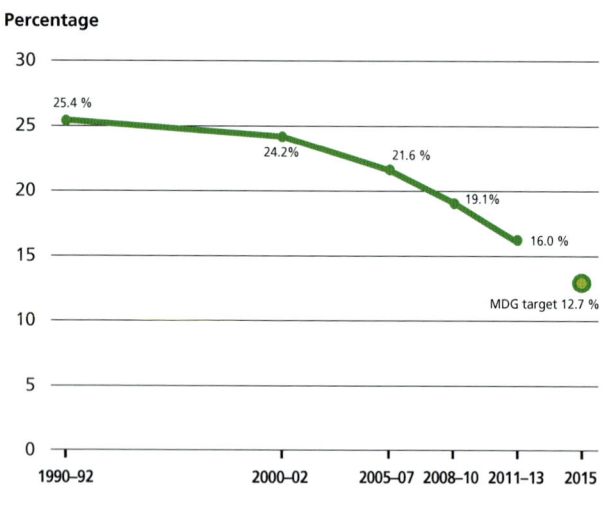

Prevalence of undernourishment

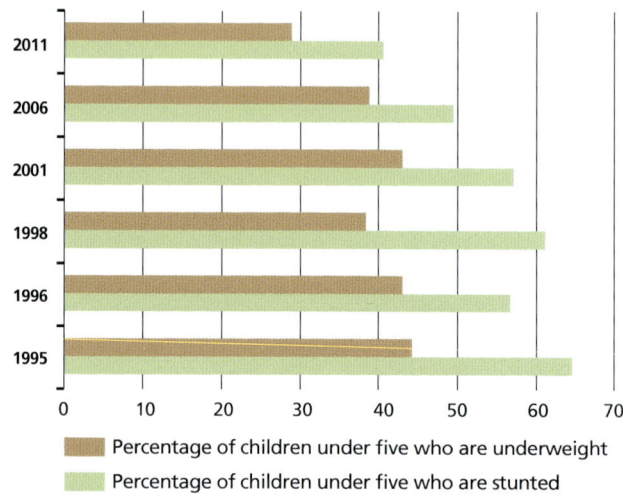

Percentage of children under five who are underweight

Percentage of children under five who are stunted

Sources: FAO (left); WHO, and Ministry of Health and Population of Nepal, 2012 (right).

FIGURE 25

Nepal has maintained and even slightly increased food availability per person since 1990–92, although food production has increased only slightly

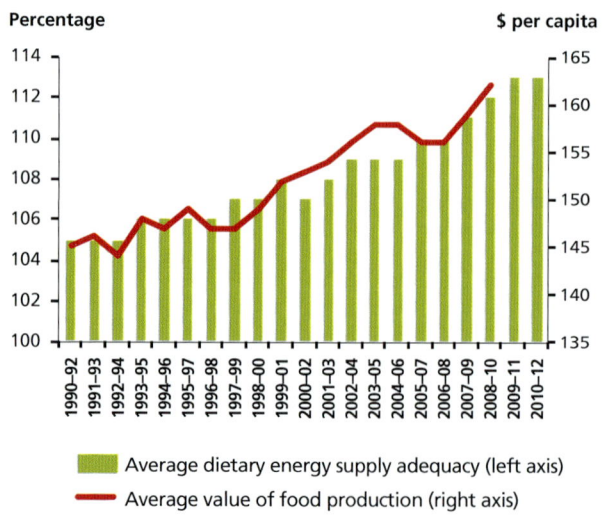

Food production and dietary energy supply adequacy

Average dietary energy supply adequacy (left axis)

Average value of food production (right axis)

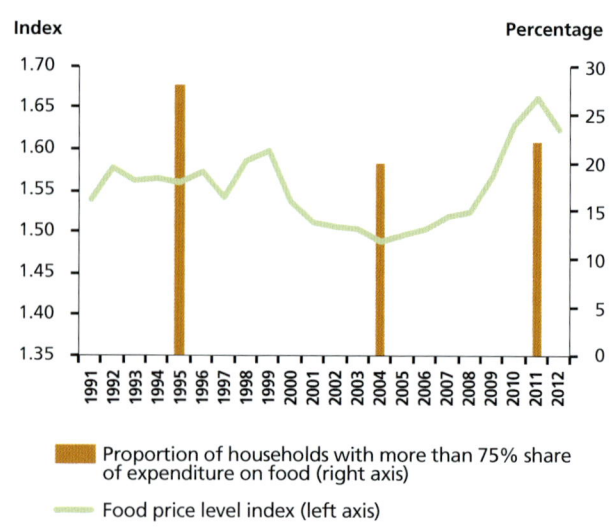

Food prices and household food expenditure

Proportion of households with more than 75% share of expenditure on food (right axis)

Food price level index (left axis)

Note: Average value of food production denominated in 2004–06 international prices.
Sources: FAO (left); National Planning Commission and Central Bureau of Statistics, 2013 (right).

Given that there is enough food in the country, undernourishment is mainly caused by problems in economic access. At the national level, Nepal has met the MDG poverty target, having reduced extreme poverty rates from 68 percent in 1996 to 25 percent in 2010. Nevertheless, the country is still one of the poorest in the world.

However, reduction in poverty, and therefore hunger, in Nepal is not so much the result of the development of Nepal's economy but of a large increase in remittances from migrant workers; in 2011–12 these amounted to 23 percent of GDP.[21] While remittance income has helped significantly reduce poverty and food insecurity, the migration on which it is based has adversely affected agricultural productivity, as those who out-migrate are usually the male members of farm families. Women are left to do all the farm management and labour on their own. It is estimated that around 30 percent of the poor are in female-headed households, most of them engaged in agriculture. Given this important role of women in food production, policies should be put in place to enable them to enhance productivity and to encourage efficient use of remittances for investment.

Progress in the fight against poverty and hunger has been extremely uneven across the country. For example, in 2010 the incidence of poverty ranged from 9 percent of the urban population in the Hills region to 42 percent of the rural population in the Mountains region.[22] Economic and physical constraints to access to food render many households unable to acquire enough food to meet their minimum needs. Physical constraints are significant. Nepal has few roads, and most of these are of poor quality: the country's road density in 2008 was about 13.5 kilometres per 100 square kilometres of land area, as compared with an average of 72 kilometres per 100 square kilometres in Southern Asia as a whole. In remote areas there are few markets and commodity prices are high because of high transportation costs. For example, rice in difficult-to-access regions can cost three times as much as in Terai, a region bordering India and the most productive agricultural zone in the country.[23]

Food security varies across the country. In the Mountains region, staples provide more than 75 percent of calories in 60 percent of households, compared with only 13 percent of households in urban Kathmandu. Lack of diversity in diets results in undernutrition being prevalent even among children younger than six months of age, suggesting that poor nutrition constrains growth even before birth. Indeed, maternal undernutrition is a serious problem in Nepal: 35 percent of women of reproductive age and 46 percent of children are anaemic.[24]

With food prices in the country increasing since 2004, poor and food-insecure households have become more and more food-insecure as high food prices have put increasing stress on family budgets. On average, households in Nepal spend 60 percent of their income on food; poor and very poor households spend an even larger proportion on food. Almost a quarter of the population, mostly rural, allocates more than 75 percent of their budget to food, making them extremely vulnerable to price spikes such as those experienced since 2008.

● ●

Nicaragua: Economic and political stability and sound policies addressing smallholders and the vulnerable pay off

Since the early 1990s, the adequacy of average dietary energy supply has increased steadily in Nicaragua while the prevalence of undernourishment fell from 55 percent in 1990–92 to less than 22 percent in 2011–13 (Figure 26). Nicaragua achieved the 2015 MDG hunger target between 2000–02 and 2005–07. However, this is no reason for complacency as the current prevalence of undernourishment is still a high 22 percent.

Much of this progress is the result of the period of economic and political stability experienced after several years of political and economic turmoil in the 1980s and a succession of costly natural disasters. This stability allowed the government to shift the focus from short-term emergency relief to long-term development and poverty-targeting plans.

Well-targeted policies, diversified food production, increased access to new international markets through participation in the Central America Free Trade Agreement and, at least for some periods, beneficial terms of trade partially cushioned the effects of the natural disasters and allowed the agriculture sector to start developing. The per capita value of food production has increased by 68 percent since 1990–92, bringing dietary energy supply adequacy above 100 percent by the beginning of the new millennium (Figure 26). Increased supplies of beans and vegetables have raised the daily average protein supply from 46 grams per capita in 1990–92 to 65 grams per capita in 2007–09.

Most of Nicaragua's agriculture is small scale, labour intensive and characterized by constraints in raising its productivity. The proportion of arable land equipped for irrigation remains extremely low (3.2 percent in 2007–09) and adoption of more modern productive technologies is hampered by low incomes, low educational levels and

FIGURE **26**

Nicaragua achieved its MDG hunger target before 2005–07 and achieved dietary energy sufficiency around year 2000

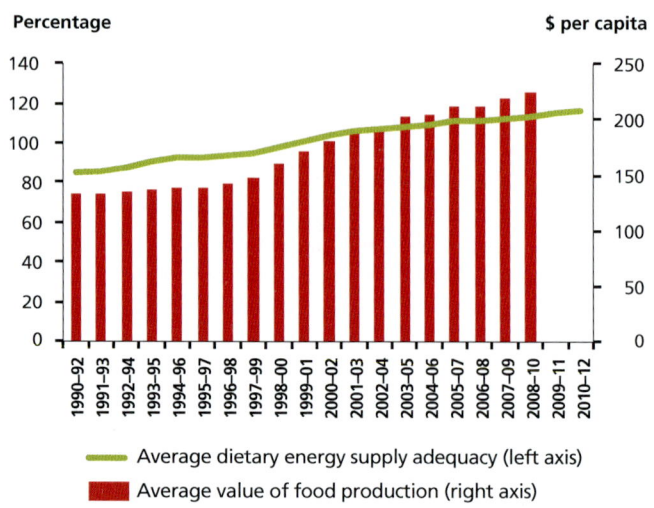

Prevalence of undernourishment

Percentage

55.1%
31.2%
25.5%
23.1%
21.7%
MDG target 27.5%

1990–92   2000–02   2005–07   2008–10   2011–13   2015

Food production and dietary energy supply adequacy

Percentage   **$ per capita**

1990-92 1991-93 1992-94 1993-95 1994-96 1995-97 1996-98 1997-99 1998-00 1999-01 2000-02 2001-03 2002-04 2003-05 2004-06 2005-07 2006-08 2007-09 2008-10 2009-11 2010-12

━━━ Average dietary energy supply adequacy (left axis)
▉▉▉ Average value of food production (right axis)

Note: Average value of food production denominated in 2004–06 international prices.
Source: FAO.

limited access to credit. In an effort to overcome these constraints, the government has developed programmes such as the Agro-seeds Programme which promotes technology transfer and the Productive Food Programme which has given about 75 000 poor rural households access to land and other productive assets, such as animals, seeds and fertilizer.[25]

Economic growth since the early 1990s has been insufficient to reduce poverty levels substantially, but some progress was registered after 2005 thanks to higher growth rates and an improved distribution of income.[26] In 2005, 32 percent of the population still lived on $2 a day or less (Figure 27). Poverty rates differed markedly between regions and were up to four times as high in rural areas as in urban areas. The proportion of people living in extreme poverty ($1.25 per day or less) declined from 18 percent in 1993 to 12 percent in 2005. If this rate of decline continues, the country is on track to meet the MDG target of halving the prevalence of extreme poverty by 2015. Despite the widespread poverty, the enhancement of agricultural productivity, especially that of smallholder farmers, and the resultant increase in the availability of food has contributed significantly to reducing the prevalence of hunger. Article 69 of Nicaragua's Constitution makes explicit provisions for the right of people to be protected against hunger and the role of the state to promote availability of food and equitable access to it. In 2009, Parliament passed a Food and Nutrition Security and Sovereignty Law, establishing the institutional and governance framework for food security and nutrition in order to protect and guarantee people's right to adequate food, define the mechanisms for intersectoral and

multistakeholder coordination and the main policy areas to be addressed.[27]

Prevalence of undernutrition has declined since 1990 but 23 percent of children under five years old were recorded as stunted in 2007, albeit down from nearly 30 percent in 1993 (Figure 27).

Marked differences are observed in nutritional levels depending on income group and geographic location, reflecting variations in access to antenatal and child care and to adequate sanitation. The government has put in place a number of programmes to address these problems, such as the *Red de Protección Social*. This conditional cash transfer programme implemented from 2000 to 2006 resulted in a five percentage point decline in stunting in under-fives after just two years of implementation.[28]

Nicaragua's geographical position and geomorphology make it especially vulnerable to natural disasters. Over the last 30 years, storms, floods and other disasters have killed more than 4 000 people and caused much economic loss. Poor farming households, most of which are reliant on rainfed agriculture, are particularly vulnerable to disasters and unpredictable weather. Lessons have been learned, however, and disasters in the 2000s have caused much less economic damage than those in the 1980s or 1990s. Nicaragua's comprehensive and multisectoral approach to disaster risk management includes programmes that help households cope with the immediate effects of disasters, but also offer them the option to be involved in new and more economically rewarding opportunities that have long-term impact on their earnings and increase their resilience to weather shocks.[29]

FIGURE **27**

Nicaragua's GDP has increased steadily since 1993 and prevalence of poverty and undernutrition have declined

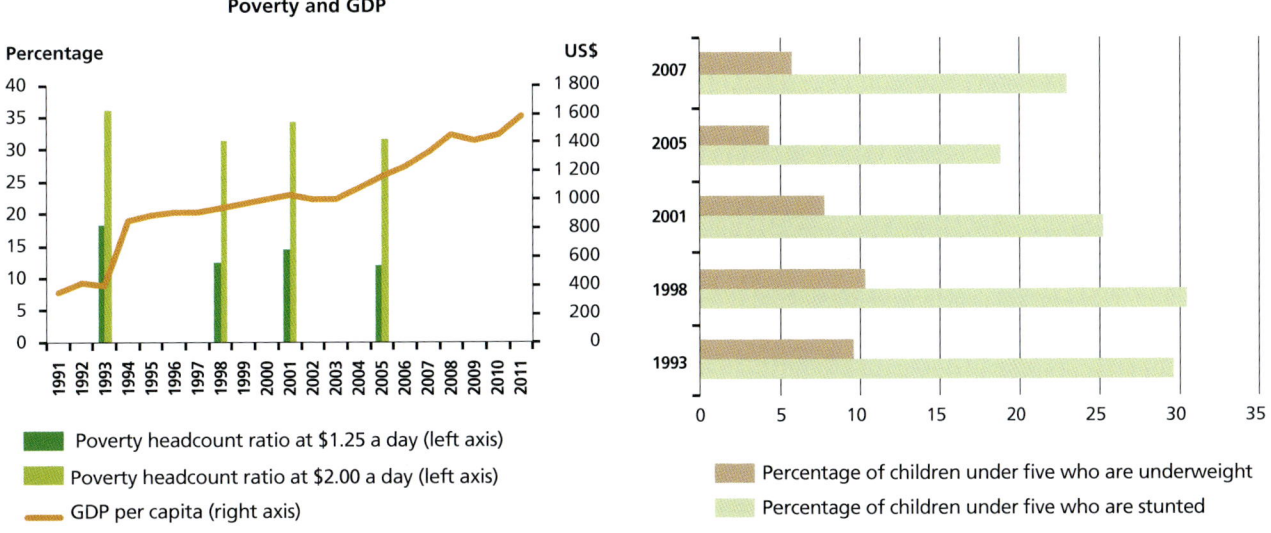

Poverty and GDP

Note: Poverty thresholds denominated in 2005 international prices.
Sources: World Development Indicators, 2012 (left); WHO (right).

Tajikistan: Structural changes in agriculture are needed to create resilience against external shocks and programmes are needed to ensure adequate diets for the vulnerable

During the 1990s, Tajikistan, a landlocked country in Central Asia, experienced a difficult transition from a centrally-planned to a market economy and a civil war from 1992 to 1997, resulting in little progress in reducing poverty and hunger (Figure 28). However, the economy grew by up to 9 percent per year between 2000 and 2008 as a result of improved policies, public investment, donor assistance, a favourable external environment, with high world prices for the country's main exports (cotton and aluminium), and increasing remittances from migrants. Nevertheless, Tajikistan remains one of the poorest countries in the region, with GDP per capita only recently recovering to a level comparable with pre-war levels in real terms.

Although progress in reducing undernourishment since the early 2000s has been good, almost one in three people is still chronically undernourished according to the most recent estimate. Since 1999, the percentage of children who are stunted has declined only marginally, reflecting sustained periods of undernutrition (Figure 28). The country's main challenges remain addressing long-term agricultural development needs, and achieving the high and sustainable levels of economic growth necessary to reduce poverty and hunger.

During the 1990s, agricultural production was severely affected by the civil war and the dismantling of the centrally-planned economy, but since the early 2000s it has increased by nearly 6 percent per year. Most of the increase was the result of productivity gains in the private farm sector and on household plots, which together account for some 82 percent of agricultural land in Tajikistan (59 percent on private farms and 23 percent on household plots).[30] By 2006, family-run household plots were producing 50 percent of the country's crops and 94 percent of its aggregate livestock output.

Delays in reforming the agriculture sector and lack of clarity concerning property rights weakened incentives for farmers to invest and increase agricultural productivity. Currently, the reform process is being deepened by shifting local authorities' functions away from intervening in farm activities and production decisions and towards helping farmers to respond to price signals through the provision of information, training and development of agricultural input markets and rural finance.[31]

Vigorous and sustained economic growth since 2000 has led to a fivefold increase in GDP per capita (albeit from an extremely low base of US$178 in 1999). This, together with large increases in remittances over the same period, resulted in a large decline in extreme poverty, from over half of the population in 1999 to about 6.5 percent in 2009 (Figure 29). Progress in poverty reduction is, however, very uneven over the various regions within the country. Partly as a result of

FIGURE 28

Tajikistan has made little progress in reducing prevalence of undernourishment and underweight

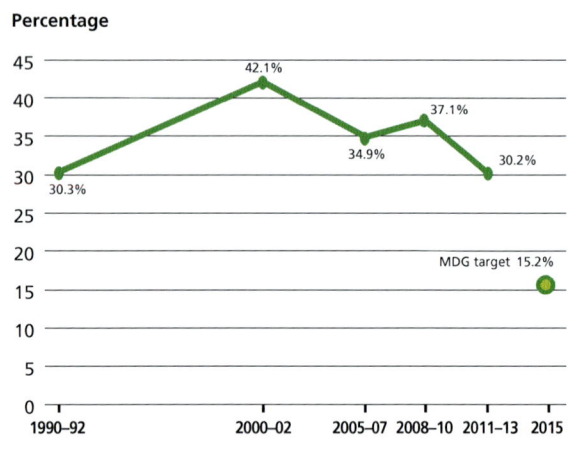

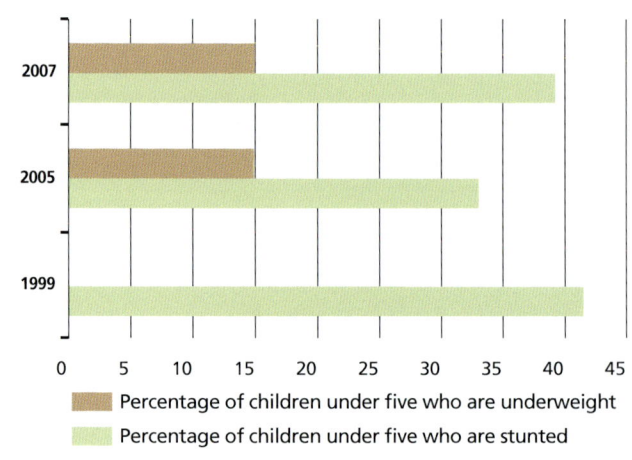

Sources: FAO (left); WHO (right).

FIGURE 29

Tajikistan's GDP has grown rapidly since 2000, with a rapid decline in the proportion of people living in extreme poverty. Remittances also increased rapidly over the same period

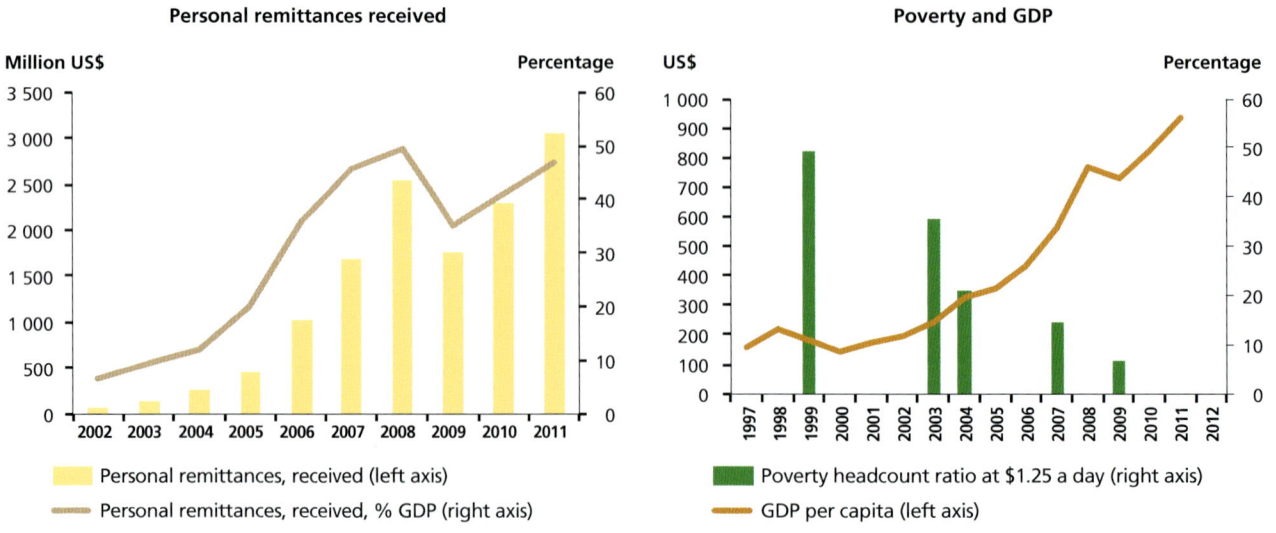

Note: Poverty threshold denominated in 2005 international prices.
Source: World Development Indicators, 2012.

incomplete land reform, high rates of poverty still prevail in rural areas; in several regions about half of the people were still poor in 2009 and more that 15 percent lived below the extreme poverty threshold, with limited access to nutritious food.[32]

Poor transport infrastructure, especially in mountainous regions, limits access to nutritious food in many parts of the country. Poor children derive about 60 percent of their calorie intake from bread and flour products and 16 percent from fats and oils, with meat and vegetables providing a mere 2 percent and 6 percent, respectively. Lack of dietary diversity results in widespread vitamin and mineral deficiencies; these can have serious and long-lasting consequences for individual welfare and for the country's socio-economic development.

As a result of the low productivity of its agriculture, Tajikistan depends heavily on food imports. According to the most recent estimate, the country imports about half of the cereals it consumes, and the cost of food imports is absorbing a gradually increasing share of total merchandise export revenue. The global economic recession that followed the food price surge in 2007–08 resulted in a temporary but significant decline in the inflow of remittances, which accounted for nearly half of Tajikistan's GDP in 2008, and a fall in export earnings from cotton and aluminium, the country's two main exports. The resultant decrease in both national and household income seriously hampered progress towards poverty reduction and food security (Figure 29). Remittances have since increased again, reaching 50 percent of GDP in 2011, sustaining the fight against poverty and hunger. However, this underlines the country's vulnerability to external shocks.

Uganda: Sluggish growth in agricultural productivity results in setbacks

Since the early 2000s, the prevalence of undernourishment in Uganda has been increasing and the country is unlikely to achieve the MDG hunger target by 2015 (Figure 30). The upward trend in the prevalence of undernourishment is the result of growth in food production failing to keep up with population growth, which, with an annual rate of more than 3.2 percent, is among the highest in the world.

Food production per capita has been declining since 2002–04 (Figure 30).[33] Dietary energy supply, which includes the energy supplied by imported food, has also declined since 2003–05, but remains – on average – adequate to meet the energy requirements of the population. However, unequal distribution and access to food mean that almost one-third of the population remains chronically undernourished.

The low productivity growth in Ugandan agriculture is, at least partly, the result of the limited use of modern technology and inputs. Given the country's high population density –173 people per square kilometre – intensive methods of farming are becoming increasingly necessary. To tackle this challenge the government has initiated a number of policies aimed at facilitating the adoption of modern technologies by smallholder farmers. For example, the National Agricultural Advisory Services programme, a public–private approach to extension service delivery, has been successful in promoting adoption of improved varieties of crops and some other yield-enhancing technologies.[34]

Under the Comprehensive Africa Agriculture Development Programme, the Government of Uganda has committed itself to increasing public spending on agriculture to 10 percent of the national budget. In 2010–11, however, government spending on agriculture amounted to only 5 percent, down from 7.6 percent in the previous year.[35] If Uganda is to realize its agricultural potential, the government must provide public goods such as extension services and irrigation, transport and communication infrastructure to allow smallholder farmers, who account for over 95 percent of all farms, to increase their productivity. Increasing agricultural productivity will not only contribute towards increased food security, but will also allow the country to produce a surplus, particularly of cereals, for export to food-deficit regions in Africa.

Per capita food production is much more variable in Uganda than the average for sub-Saharan Africa, largely because of limited use of irrigation (Figure 31). With less than 1 percent of the land being irrigated, Ugandan agriculture relies almost exclusively on rainfed production. Crop yields, and therefore prices, reflect fluctuations in rainfall.

Over the last decade, the country has seen an increase in the variability of rainfall and a higher frequency of extreme climate events. For example, the 2010–11 rainfall deficits caused an estimated loss of US$1.2 billion or 7.5 percent of the country's GDP. In the north-eastern Karamoja region, consecutive years of poor weather conditions and below-

FIGURE **30**

FIGURE **30**

Prevalence of undernourishment in Uganda has increased since 2000–02, and food production per person is declining, as is adequacy of dietary energy supply

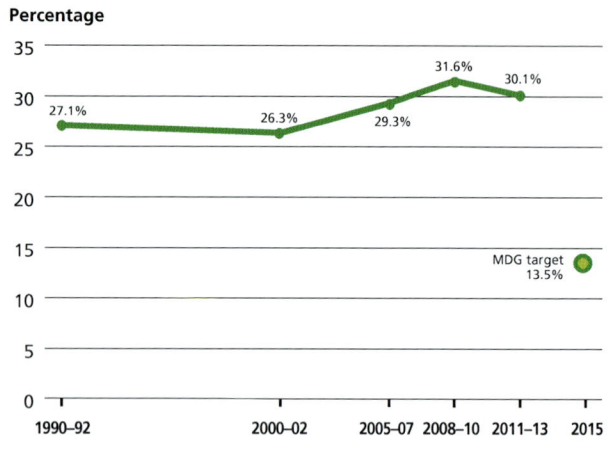

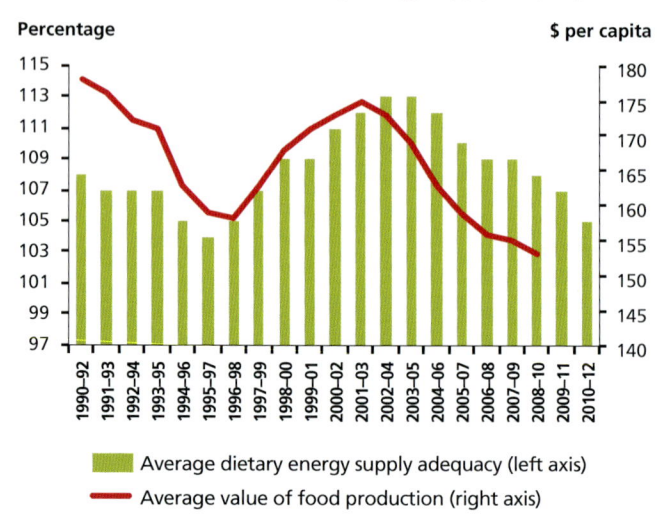

Note: Average value of food production denominated in 2004–06 international prices.
Source: FAO.

FIGURE **31**

GDP is increasing in Uganda and the country is on track to meet the MDG poverty target by 2015, but per capita food production is highly variable

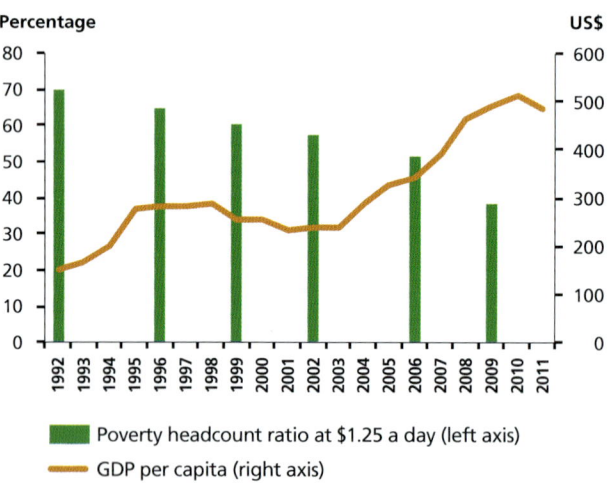

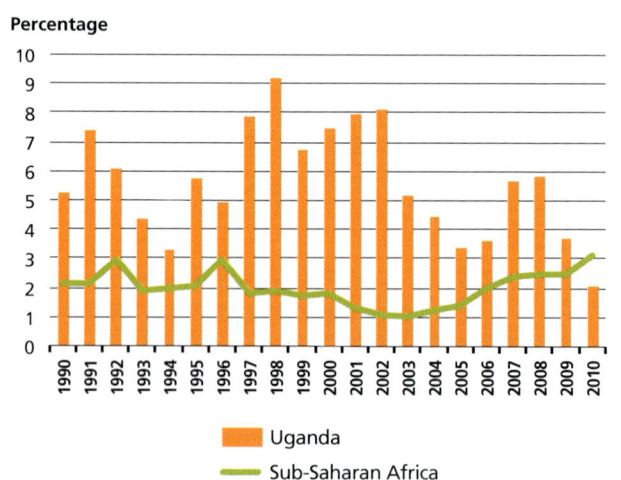

Notes: Poverty threshold denominated in 2005 international prices. For the definition of per capita food production variability, see the Food Security Indicators available at http://www.fao.org/economic/ess/ess-fs/fs-data/en/.
Sources: World Development Indicators, 2012, and Uganda Bureau of Statistics (left); FAO (right).

normal rainfall have had a strong and adverse impact on food security due to crop failure and low livestock productivity.[36]

Although the country is on track to meet the MDG target of halving the proportion of people in extreme poverty, 38 percent of the population was still living on $1.25 a day or less in 2009 (Figure 31).

Food insecurity is more prevalent in rural areas than in urban areas and considerable differences are observed across the country. Since 1997, government expenditure on health care has increased, with more people, especially the poorest, using government health centres.[37] Better health care and child care practices, together with reductions in poverty and improvements in water and sanitation under the government's Poverty Eradication Action Plan, have contributed towards improved nutrition in recent years.[38] The percentage of stunted children declined from 44.8 percent in 2001 to 33.4 percent in 2011, and the prevalence of underweight children decreased from 21.5 percent in 1995 to 13.8 percent in 2011.

Regional differences in nutrition outcomes are significant. Across regions, high rates of poverty and poor access to clean water and sanitation are reflected in high undernutrition rates; in Karamoja, for example, in 2011, 32 percent of children under five years of age were underweight, compared with only 6 percent in Kampala, the country's capital.

Key messages

- Policies aimed at enhancing agricultural productivity and increasing food availability, especially when smallholders are targeted, can achieve hunger reduction even where poverty is widespread. When they are combined with social protection and other measures that increase the incomes of poor families to buy food, they can have an even more positive impact and spur rural development, by creating vibrant markets and employment opportunities, making possible equitable economic growth.

- Remittances, which have globally become three times larger than official development assistance, have had significant impacts on poverty and food security. This report suggests that remittances can help to reduce poverty, leading to reduced hunger, better diets and, given appropriate policies, increased on-farm investment.

- Long-term commitment to mainstreaming food security and nutrition in public policies and programmes is key to hunger reduction. Keeping food security and agriculture high on the development agenda, through comprehensive reforms, improvements in the investment climate, supported by sustained social protection, is crucial for achieving major reductions in poverty and undernourishment.

Annex 1

TABLE A1.1
Prevalence of undernourishment and progress towards the World Food Summit (WFS)[1] and the Millennium Development Goal (MDG)[2] targets in developing regions

Regions/subregions/countries	Number of people undernourished							Proportion of undernourished in total population						
	1990–1992	2000–2002	2005–2007	2008–2010	2011–2013[3]	Change so far[4]	Progress towards WFS target[5]	1990–1992	2000–2002	2005–2007	2008–2010	2011–2013[3]	Change so far[4]	Progress towards MDG target[5]
	(millions)					(%)		(%)						
WORLD[6]	1 015.3	957.3	906.6	878.2	842.3	−17.0	▼	18.9	15.5	13.8	12.9	12.0	−36.5	🟨
Developed regions	19.8	18.4	13.6	15.2	15.7	20.7	na	<5	<5	<5	<5	<5	na	na
Developing regions	995.5	938.9	892.9	863.0	826.6	−17.0	▼	23.6	18.8	16.7	15.5	14.3	−39.3	🟨
Least-developed countries[7]	201.9	245.4	246.3	252.4	252.1	24.9	▲	38.6	36.2	32.4	31.0	29.0	−24.8	🟨
Landlocked developing countries[8]	95.7	117.4	112.1	110.0	107.7	12.6	▲	35.6	34.7	29.8	27.4	25.2	−29.4	🟨
Small island developing states[9]	10.3	9.7	9.9	9.2	9.8	−5.3	▼	24.8	20.4	19.3	17.5	17.9	−27.7	🟨
Low income economies[10]	193.0	241.0	236.6	240.8	235.4	22.0	▲	37.5	36.6	32.2	30.9	28.3	−24.5	🟨
Lower-middle-income economies[11]	436.8	438.6	419.1	406.4	384.7	−11.9	▼	24.3	20.3	17.9	16.6	15.0	−38.3	🟨
Low-income food-deficit countries[12]	531.5	591.5	579.5	576.2	554.9	4.4	◄►	27.2	24.6	22.0	20.8	19.0	−30.2	🟨
FAO regions														
Africa[13]	*173.1*	*209.5*	*212.8*	*221.6*	*222.7*	*28.7*	▲	*32.7*	*30.6*	*27.5*	*26.6*	*24.8*	*−24.2*	🟨
Asia and the Pacific[14]	*735.0*	*643.6*	*599.3*	*562.7*	*528.7*	*−28.1*	▼	*20.9*	*16.0*	*14.1*	*12.9*	*11.8*	*−43.2*	🟨
Europe and Central Asia[15]	*10.0*	*12.3*	*8.0*	*7.7*	*6.1*	*39.1*	▼	*8.2*	*9.0*	*5.6*	*5.2*	*<5*	*na*	🟩
Latin America and the Caribbean[16]	*65.6*	*61.0*	*54.6*	*50.3*	*47.0*	*−28.4*	▼	*14.7*	*11.7*	*9.8*	*8.7*	*7.9*	*−46.6*	🟨
Near East and North Africa[17]	*25.8*	*29.9*	*37.2*	*41.2*	*43.7*	*69.4*	▲	*9.0*	*9.0*	*10.0*	*10.0*	*10.0*	*11.1*	🟥
AFRICA	177.6	214.3	217.6	226.0	226.4	27.5	▲	27.3	25.9	23.4	22.7	21.2	−22.3	🟨
Northern Africa	4.6	4.9	4.8	4.4	3.7	−19.6	▼	<5	<5	<5	<5	<5	−41.8	🟨
Algeria	1.4	1.9	1.6	ns	ns	na	na	5.5	6.1	<5	<5	<5	na	🟩
Egypt	ns	ns	ns	ns	ns	na	na	<5	<5	<5	<5	<5	na	🟩
Libya	ns	ns	ns	ns	ns	na	na	<5	<5	<5	<5	<5	na	🟩
Morocco	1.7	1.9	1.6	1.7	ns	−4.0	◄►	6.7	6.4	5.3	5.3	<5	na	🟩
Tunisia	ns	ns	ns	ns	ns	na	na	<5	<5	<5	<5	<5	na	🟩
Sub-Saharan Africa[18]	173.1	209.5	212.8	221.6	222.7	28.7	▲	32.7	30.6	27.5	26.6	24.8	−24.2	🟨
Angola	6.7	6.8	5.9	5.8	4.9	−27.0	▼	63.2	47.4	34.8	31.4	24.4	−61.4	🟩
Benin	1.1	1.1	1.0	0.9	0.6	−48.3	▼	22.4	16.7	13.1	10.9	6.1	−72.7	🟩
Botswana	0.4	0.6	0.6	0.6	0.5	47.8	▲	25.1	35.2	33.3	32.1	25.7	2.5	🟥
Burkina Faso	2.2	3.5	3.7	3.8	4.4	99.6	▲	22.9	27.5	25.3	23.9	25.0	9.4	🟥
Burundi	2.5	4.1	5.2	5.7	5.9	131.8	▲	44.4	62.3	69.7	69.5	67.3	51.6	🟥
Cameroon	4.8	4.8	3.6	2.9	2.7	−43.1	▼	38.3	29.7	19.9	15.2	13.3	−65.2	🟩
Central African Republic	1.5	1.7	1.7	1.4	1.3	−11.6	▼	48.5	44.7	40.9	33.0	28.2	−41.9	🟨
Chad	3.7	3.6	3.8	4.1	3.5	−6.8	▼	60.1	41.8	38.0	37.2	29.4	−51.2	🟩
Congo	1.0	0.9	1.2	1.4	1.4	34.1	▲	42.4	29.4	33.8	35.0	33.0	−22.2	🟨
Côte d'Ivoire	1.7	3.6	3.4	3.8	4.2	146.1	▲	13.3	21.5	18.8	19.5	20.5	54.7	🟥

TABLE A1.1
Prevalence of undernourishment and progress towards the World Food Summit (WFS)[1] and the Millennium Development Goal (MDG)[2] targets in developing regions

Regions/subregions/countries	Number of people undernourished							Proportion of undernourished in total population						
	1990–1992	2000–2002	2005–2007	2008–2010	2011–2013[3]	Change so far[4]	Progress towards WFS target[5]	1990–1992	2000–2002	2005–2007	2008–2010	2011–2013[3]	Change so far[4]	Progress towards MDG target[5]
	(millions)					(%)		(%)						
Eritrea	2.4	2.9	3.5	3.5	3.4	43.8	▲	75.0	77.0	74.7	69.4	61.3	–18.2	🟨
Ethiopia	35.5	36.0	34.5	33.2	32.1	–9.6	▼	71.0	53.5	45.4	40.9	37.1	–47.7	🟩
Gabon	0.1	0.1	0.1	0.1	0.1	–5.0	◀▶	9.5	6.5	5.8	6.2	5.6	–41.7	🟨
Gambia	0.2	0.3	0.3	0.2	0.3	61.1	▲	18.2	20.0	19.8	12.0	16.0	–11.7	🟨
Ghana	6.8	3.3	2.1	1.4	ns	na	na	44.4	16.8	9.6	5.8	<5	na	🟩
Guinea	1.1	1.7	1.6	1.5	1.6	43.3	▲	18.2	20.6	17.1	15.3	15.2	–16.6	🟨
Kenya	8.4	10.9	10.1	10.9	11.0	30.6	▲	34.8	33.9	27.5	27.5	25.8	–26.0	🟨
Lesotho	0.3	0.3	0.3	0.4	0.3	22.4	▲	17.0	17.4	16.4	17.3	15.7	–7.8	🟨
Liberia	0.6	1.0	1.0	1.1	1.2	96.3	▲	29.6	34.4	29.4	29.4	28.6	–3.2	🟨
Madagascar	2.8	5.4	5.2	6.0	6.0	110.6	▲	24.4	33.8	28.5	29.7	27.2	11.6	🟥
Malawi	4.3	3.1	3.3	3.3	3.2	–26.1	▼	45.2	26.7	24.7	23.1	20.0	–55.6	🟩
Mali	2.2	2.5	2.0	1.4	1.2	–45.8	▼	24.9	21.7	15.0	9.3	7.3	–70.5	🟩
Mauritania	0.3	0.3	0.3	0.3	0.3	6.4	▲	12.9	9.7	8.9	7.8	7.8	–39.8	🟨
Mauritius	0.1	0.1	0.1	0.1	0.1	–23.4	▼	8.6	6.5	5.9	5.8	5.4	–37.4	🟨
Mozambique	8.0	8.4	8.6	9.1	9.0	12.0	▲	57.8	44.8	40.4	39.7	36.8	–36.4	🟨
Namibia	0.5	0.5	0.6	0.7	0.7	31.0	▲	36.2	24.8	27.1	33.3	29.3	–18.9	🟨
Niger	2.9	2.9	2.8	1.9	2.3	–19.1	▼	35.5	26.0	20.5	13.0	13.9	–60.9	🟩
Nigeria	21.3	13.7	10.8	10.7	12.1	–43.0	▼	21.3	10.8	7.5	6.9	7.3	–65.8	🟩
Rwanda	3.6	3.8	4.0	3.5	3.4	–5.9	▼	52.3	45.3	41.9	34.1	29.7	–43.2	🟨
Senegal	1.6	2.4	1.9	1.9	2.8	72.6	▲	22.0	24.7	16.8	15.9	21.6	–1.7	🟨
Sierra Leone	1.7	1.8	1.9	1.9	1.8	6.2	▲	42.5	41.3	35.3	33.6	29.4	–30.9	🟨
South Africa	ns	ns	ns	ns	ns	na	na	<5	<5	<5	<5	<5	na	🟩
South Sudan*														
Sudan*														
Sudan (former)*	11.4	9.7	12.5	15.3	na	na	na	41.9	27.7	31.7	36.1	na	na	na
Swaziland	0.1	0.2	0.2	0.3	0.4	212.7	▲	15.8	17.8	19.1	27.8	35.8	127.1	🟥
Togo	1.3	1.3	1.1	1.2	1.0	–25.0	▼	34.8	25.6	20.5	20.5	15.5	–55.3	🟩
Uganda	5.0	6.6	8.6	10.2	10.7	115.9	▲	27.1	26.3	29.3	31.6	30.1	11.0	🟥
United Republic of Tanzania	7.6	14.4	14.2	15.9	15.7	107.1	▲	28.8	41.3	35.6	36.5	33.0	14.5	🟥
Zambia	2.7	4.7	5.7	6.0	6.0	119.4	▲	33.8	45.4	48.9	47.1	43.1	27.4	🟥
Zimbabwe	4.7	5.5	4.7	4.3	4.0	–15.3	▼	43.6	43.6	37.9	34.0	30.5	–30.2	🟨
ASIA	**751.3**	**662.3**	**619.6**	**585.5**	**552.0**	**–26.5**	**▼**	**24.1**	**18.3**	**16.1**	**14.7**	**13.5**	**–44.1**	🟨
Caucasus and Central Asia[19]	**9.7**	**11.6**	**7.3**	**7.0**	**5.5**	**–43.0**	**▼**	**14.4**	**16.2**	**9.8**	**9.2**	**7.0**	**–51.4**	🟩
Armenia	0.8	0.6	0.2	ns	ns	na	na	24.0	20.2	5.3	<5	<5	na	🟩

Annex 1

TABLE A1.1
Prevalence of undernourishment and progress towards the World Food Summit (WFS)[1] and the Millennium Development Goal (MDG)[2] targets in developing regions

Regions/subregions/countries	Number of people undernourished							Proportion of undernourished in total population						
	1990–1992	2000–2002	2005–2007	2008–2010	2011–2013[3]	Change so far[4]	Progress towards WFS target[5]	1990–1992	2000–2002	2005–2007	2008–2010	2011–2013[3]	Change so far[4]	Progress towards MDG target[5]
	(millions)					(%)		(%)						
Azerbaijan	1.7	0.8	ns	ns	ns	na	na	23.8	10.1	<5	<5	<5	na	■
Kazakhstan	ns	1.2	ns	ns	ns	na	na	<5	8	<5	<5	<5	na	■
Kyrgyzstan	0.8	0.9	0.5	0.5	0.3	−58.9	▼˙	17.7	17.6	9.7	9.3	5.9	−66.5	■
Tajikistan	1.6	2.6	2.3	2.5	2.1	30.1	▲	30.3	42.1	34.9	37.1	30.2	−0.5	■
Turkmenistan	0.3	0.4	0.3	ns	ns	na	na	9.2	8.4	5.7	<5	<5	na	■
Uzbekistan	ns	3.9	2.5	2.2	1.6	na	na	<5	15.7	9.7	8.1	5.7	na	■
Eastern Asia	**278.7**	**193.5**	**184.8**	**169.1**	**166.6**	**−40.2**	**▼**	**22.2**	**14.0**	**13.0**	**11.7**	**11.4**	**−48.7**	■
Eastern Asia (excluding China)	**6.5**	**9.9**	**10.0**	**10.9**	**8.6**	**31.7**	**▲**	**9.9**	**13.9**	**13.6**	**14.6**	**11.3**	**14.5**	■
China	272.1	183.5	174.8	158.1	158.0	−41.9	▼	22.9	14.0	13.0	11.6	11.4	−50.2	■
of which Taiwan Province of China	ns	ns	1.3	1.6	1.5	na	na	<5	<5	5.6	6.7	6.3	35.3	■
Democratic People's Republic of Korea	4.8	8.4	8.6	9.7	7.6	57.0	▲	23.7	36.6	36.0	40.2	31.0	30.9	■
Mongolia	0.9	0.9	0.8	0.7	0.6	−29.3	▼	38.4	35.6	31.4	26.4	21.2	−44.7	■
Republic of Korea	ns	ns	ns	ns	ns	na	na	<5	<5	<5	<5	<5	na	■
Southern Asia[20]	**314.3**	**330.2**	**316.6**	**309.9**	**294.7**	**−6.2**	**▼**	**25.7**	**22.2**	**19.7**	**18.5**	**16.8**	**−34.6**	■
Southern Asia (excluding India)	**87.0**	**89.5**	**83.4**	**81.3**	**81.0**	**−6.9**	**▼**	**26.3**	**21.6**	**18.5**	**17.2**	**16.4**	**−37.8**	■
Bangladesh	36.5	22.7	21.6	22.8	24.8	−32.2	▼	33.9	17.2	15.1	15.5	16.3	−52.1	■
India	227.3	240.7	233.1	228.6	213.8	−6.0	▼	25.5	22.5	20.1	18.9	17.0	−33.3	■
Iran (Islamic Republic of)	ns	ns	4.2	3.8	ns	na	na	<5	<5	6.0	5.2	<5	na	■
Nepal	5.0	6.1	6.0	5.6	5.0	0.2	◄►	25.4	24.2	21.6	19.1	16.0	−36.8	■
Pakistan	31.2	37.5	34.3	32.5	31.0	−0.6	◄►	27.2	25.4	21.2	19.0	17.2	−36.5	■
Sri Lanka	5.9	5.5	5.4	5.2	4.8	−17.3	▼	33.4	28.9	27.0	25.1	22.8	−31.7	■
South-Eastern Asia[21]	**140.3**	**113.6**	**94.2**	**80.5**	**64.5**	**−54.0**	**▼˙**	**31.1**	**21.5**	**16.8**	**13.8**	**10.7**	**−65.5**	■
Cambodia	3.9	4.1	3.3	2.9	2.2	−42.5	▼	39.4	32.3	24.2	20.8	15.4	−60.8	■
Indonesia	41.6	42.8	38.3	30.3	22.3	−46.3	▼	22.2	19.8	16.7	12.8	9.1	−58.9	■
Lao People's Democratic Republic	1.9	2.1	1.9	1.7	1.7	−11.6	▼	44.7	38.1	32.3	28.3	26.7	−40.2	■
Malaysia	ns	ns	ns	ns	ns	na	na	<5	<5	<5	<5	<5	na	■
Philippines	15.5	16.9	15.9	15.1	15.6	0.8	◄►	24.5	21.3	18.2	16.5	16.2	−34.1	■
Thailand	25.0	10.8	6.4	6.3	4.0	−83.9	▼˙	43.3	16.9	9.5	9.2	5.8	−86.7	■
Viet Nam	33.1	14.4	11.7	10.3	7.4	−77.6	▼˙	48.3	18.0	13.9	11.8	8.3	−82.9	■
Western Asia[22]	**8.4**	**13.5**	**16.8**	**19.1**	**20.6**	**144.9**	**▲**	**6.6**	**8.3**	**9.2**	**9.7**	**9.8**	**49.1**	■
Iraq	1.8	4.8	7.0	8.0	8.8	394.4	▲	10.0	19.7	24.8	26.0	26.2	162.3	■
Jordan	0.2	0.3	ns	ns	ns	na	na	6.1	6.3	<5	<5	<5	na	■
Kuwait	0.8	ns	ns	ns	ns	na	na	39.3	<5	<5	<5	<5	na	■
Lebanon	ns	ns	ns	ns	ns	na	na	<5	<5	<5	<5	<5	na	■
Saudi Arabia	ns	ns	ns	ns	ns	na	na	<5	<5	<5	<5	<5	na	■
Syrian Arab Republic	ns	ns	ns	ns	1.3	na	na	<5	<5	<5	<5	6.0	28.1	■

TABLE A1.1
Prevalence of undernourishment and progress towards the World Food Summit (WFS)[1] and the Millennium Development Goal (MDG)[2] targets in developing regions

Regions/subregions/countries	Number of people undernourished							Proportion of undernourished in total population						
	1990–1992	2000–2002	2005–2007	2008–2010	2011–2013[3]	Change so far[4]	Progress towards WFS target[5]	1990–1992	2000–2002	2005–2007	2008–2010	2011–2013[3]	Change so far[4]	Progress towards MDG target[5]
	(millions)					(%)		(%)						
Turkey	ns	ns	ns	ns	ns	na	na	<5	<5	<5	<5	<5	na	🟩
United Arab Emirates	ns	ns	ns	ns	ns	na	na	<5	<5	<5	<5	<5	na	🟩
Yemen	3.7	5.8	6.9	7.6	7.4	101.4	▲	29.2	31.7	32.4	32.5	28.8	−1.1	🟨
LATIN AMERICA AND THE CARIBBEAN	**65.7**	**61.0**	**54.6**	**50.3**	**47.0**	**−28.4**	**▼**	**14.7**	**11.7**	**9.8**	**8.7**	**7.9**	**−46.6**	🟨
Caribbean[23]	**8.3**	**7.2**	**7.5**	**6.8**	**7.2**	**−13.3**	**▼**	**27.6**	**21.3**	**21.0**	**18.8**	**19.3**	**−29.9**	🟨
Cuba	0.8	ns	ns	ns	ns	na	na	7.8	<5	<5	<5	<5	na	🟩
Dominican Republic	2.4	1.8	1.7	1.6	1.6	−33.6	▼	32.5	21.0	18.3	16.2	15.6	−52.1	🟩
Haiti	4.6	4.7	5.1	4.6	5.1	11.9	▲	62.7	52.9	53.9	46.7	49.8	−20.6	🟨
Jamaica	0.2	0.2	0.2	0.2	0.2	−0.6	◀▶	10.1	7.0	7.0	8.1	8.6	−14.3	🟨
Trinidad and Tobago	0.2	0.2	0.2	0.1	0.1	−32.7	▼	12.4	12.9	13.3	11.1	7.6	−39.0	🟨
Latin America[24]	**57.4**	**53.8**	**47.2**	**43.5**	**39.8**	**−30.6**	**▼**	**13.8**	**11.0**	**9.0**	**8.0**	**7.1**	**−48.5**	🟩
Argentina	ns	ns	ns	ns	ns	na	na	<5	<5	<5	<5	<5	na	🟩
Bolivia (Plurinational State of)	2.3	2.4	2.7	2.7	2.2	−5.7	▼	33.9	28.6	29.1	28.1	21.3	−37.3	🟨
Brazil	22.8	22.0	16.7	14.4	13.6	−40.4	▼	15.0	12.5	8.9	7.5	6.9	−54.3	🟩
Chile	1.2	ns	ns	ns	ns	na	na	9.0	<5	<5	<5	<5	na	🟩
Colombia	6.9	5.3	6.1	5.7	5.1	−26.5	▼	20.3	13.2	14.0	12.5	10.6	−47.7	🟨
Costa Rica	ns	ns	ns	ns	0.4	na	na	<5	<5	<5	<5	8.2	na	🟥
Ecuador	2.8	2.7	3.0	2.8	2.4	−12.6	▼	26.4	21.2	21.7	19.6	16.3	−38.3	🟨
El Salvador	0.8	0.5	0.7	0.7	0.7	−10.0	▼	15.3	8.9	10.8	11.4	11.9	−22.2	🟨
Guatemala	1.5	2.9	4.0	4.1	4.6	198.0	▲	16.9	25.4	30.4	29.5	30.5	79.8	🟥
Guyana	0.2	0.1	0.1	0.1	0.0	−76.2	▼*	22.0	7.7	9.2	8.1	5.0	−77.2	🟩
Honduras	1.1	1.1	1.0	0.9	0.7	−37.9	▼	22.0	16.6	14.5	11.7	8.7	−60.5	🟩
Mexico	ns	ns	ns	ns	ns	na	na	<5	<5	<5	<5	<5	na	🟩
Nicaragua	2.3	1.6	1.4	1.3	1.3	−44.5	▼	55.1	31.2	25.5	23.1	21.7	−60.6	🟩
Panama	0.6	0.8	0.6	0.4	0.3	−44.9	▼	23.3	25.0	17.6	12.0	8.7	−62.5	🟩
Paraguay	0.9	0.7	0.8	1.2	1.5	69.6	▲	20.2	12.5	13.5	18.8	22.3	10.5	🟥
Peru	7.0	5.8	5.5	4.4	3.5	−49.8	▼	31.6	22.0	19.8	15.3	11.8	−62.6	🟩
Suriname	0.1	0.1	0.1	0.1	0.1	−24.2	▼	17.5	17.7	15.4	14.5	10.2	−41.4	🟨
Uruguay	0.2	ns	ns	ns	0.2	−12.5	▼	7.6	<5	<5	<5	6.2	−19.2	🟨
Venezuela (Bolivarian Republic of)	2.6	4.2	2.8	ns	ns	na	na	12.8	16.8	10.2	<5	<5	na	🟩
OCEANIA[25]	**0.8**	**1.2**	**1.1**	**1.1**	**1.2**	**42.7**	**▲**	**13.5**	**16.0**	**12.8**	**11.8**	**12.1**	**−10.5**	🟨

The prevalence of undernourishment indicator

What is the prevalence of undernourishment indicator?

The **prevalence of undernourishment (PoU)** indicator is a long-established measure, maintained by the FAO Statistics Division. The indicator was first presented in 1963, with the *Third World Food Survey* and then progressively refined.[39]

The methodology for estimating the PoU is based on the comparison of a probability distribution of *habitual* daily *dietary energy consumption*, *f(x)*, and a threshold level, called the *minimum dietary energy requirement* (MDER). Both are based on the notion of an *average individual* in the reference population.[40] Formally, the PoU is estimated as follows:

$$PoU \equiv \int_{x<MDER} f(x)\,dx \qquad (1)$$

In other words, the PoU is the probability that, after randomly selecting one individual from the population, (s)he is found to be consuming an amount of dietary energy that is insufficient to cover his or her requirement for an active and healthy life. This probability is taken as an estimate of the likely proportion of people that are undernourished in the population. An estimate of the **number of undernourished (NoU)** is then produced by multiplying the estimated PoU by the population size. The PoU and NoU have been adopted as indicators used to monitor progress towards the targets set by the Millennium Development Goals (in particular, the hunger target of MDG 1) and at the World Food Summit, respectively.

It is worth emphasizing that the probability distribution used to draw inference on the *habitual* levels of dietary energy consumption in a population, *f(x)*, refers to a typical level of daily energy consumption *during a year*. As such, *f(x)* does not reflect possible implications of insufficient food consumption levels that may prevail over shorter periods of time. If, and only if, the *average* food consumption over such a period is below requirement, the indicator would signal a condition of undernourishment.

Moreover, given that both the probability distribution *f(x)* and the threshold level in (1) are associated with the representative individual of the population – that is, a statistical construct corresponding to an individual of average age, sex, stature and physical activity level – *they do not represent, respectively, the empirical distribution of per capita food in the population* and a *threshold level that is meaningful for any actual individual in the population.*

Three frequent critiques

In recent years the FAO methodology has been exposed to three major critiques:

1. The indicator is based on a narrow definition of "hunger", covering only chronic conditions of inadequate dietary energy intake. Other aspects of food inadequacy, for example micronutrient deficiencies, are not captured.
2. The PoU indicator systematically underestimates undernourishment, as it assumes a minimum level of physical activity, typical of a sedentary lifestyle. Hence the indicator neglects the fact that many poor people are engaged in demanding physical activities.
3. The methodology is complex and based on allegedly weak macro data, whereas household surveys alone allow for a direct and more accurate measurement of undernourishment.

The first concern is indeed justified. The PoU indicator is designed to capture a clearly – and narrowly – defined concept of undernourishment, namely a state of dietary energy deprivation lasting over a year. This report is addressing this limitation by presenting and discussing measures of different dimensions of food security, through the FAO suite of food security indicators. The suite comprises numerous indicators that reflect aspects associated with the elements of a broader concept of food insecurity and hunger.

The second criticism is unfounded as the object of the criticism is actually a virtue of the methodology that is not always and not easily appreciated. As already mentioned, the FAO methodology is based on a probabilistic approach and a representative individual. Ideally, the adequacy of dietary energy intake, and thus the condition of being undernourished, would be assessed at the individual level, by comparing *individual* energy requirements with *individual* energy intake. This would allow the prevalence of undernourishment to be estimated by counting the number of people who are classified as undernourished. Such a "headcount" approach, however, is not feasible for two reasons. First, individual energy requirements are practically unobservable with standard data collection methods.[41] Second, individual food consumption cannot be measured precisely because of disparities in intra-household food allocation, the variability of individual energy requirements, and the day-to-day variability of food consumption that can arise for reasons that are independent from food insecurity (including different workloads or lifestyles, or cultural and religious habits).

Given that it is practically impossible to proceed with a headcount approach, the solution adopted by FAO has been to apply the PoU, which is an *estimator that refers to the population as a whole*, summarized by the statistical device of a "representative" individual. Obviously, when considering the population as a whole, it must be recognized that, as body weight, metabolic efficiency and physical activity levels will vary in the represented population, there is a *range* of values for energy requirements that are compatible with healthy status. It follows that only values below the minimum of such a range can be associated with undernourishment, in a probabilistic sense. Hence, for the PoU to indicate that a randomly selected individual in a population is undernourished, the appropriate threshold must be set at the lower end of the range of normal energy requirements.

The third criticism ignores the high costs of implementing surveys capable of properly estimating undernourishment for the vast majority of the countries monitored by FAO. At a minimum, hese surveys should capture food consumption at the individual level and should contain sufficient information to assess *habitual* consumption levels, as well as information on the anthropometric characteristics and activity levels of each surveyed individual that would enable the relevant individual energy requirement *threshold* to be estimated. These data requirements suggest that specific surveys, different from and more expensive than existing household surveys, would need to be designed for this purpose. By contrast, the FAO PoU methodology allows the integration of information from household surveys with macro data sources, such as food balances, censuses and demographic surveys.

Computing the PoU in practice

Estimating equation (1) requires an analytic expression for *f(x)*, and the identification of the MDER threshold.

The functional form for the probability distribution *f(x)* is chosen from a parametric family. Its characterization is obtained by estimating parameters for the *mean,* the *coefficient of variation (CV)* and the *coefficient of skewness*. Improving estimates of these parameters based on available data from various sources is a continuing endeavour of the FAO Statistics Division.

The choice of a model for the distribution

Starting with the estimates produced for the *Sixth World Food Survey* in 1996, the distribution was assumed to be lognormal. This model is very convenient from the analytic point of view, but has limited flexibility, especially in capturing the skewness of the distribution.

During the revision of the methodology conducted in 2011 and 2012, attention was drawn to the fact that raising the mean while keeping the CV constant under the lognormal distribution would result in non-negligible probability of unreasonably high levels of energy consumption. Rather, it seems more plausible that an increase in mean food consumption would make the distribution less skewed, as the relative increase in consumption among those who already consume above the average is likely to be smaller than for those consuming below the average.

The search for a more flexible model led to the adoption of the skew-normal and skew-lognormal families of distributions introduced by Azzalini,[42] with the results published in *The State of Food Insecurity in the World 2012*.

Estimating mean food consumption

To estimate per capita dietary energy consumption in a country, FAO has traditionally relied on its own food balance sheets, which are available for more than 180 countries. This choice was mainly due to a lack of suitable surveys conducted on a regular basis in most countries. Through data on production, trade and utilization of food commodities, the total amount of dietary energy available for human consumption in a country for a one-year period is derived using food composition data, allowing computation of per capita dietary energy supply (DES).

During the revision conducted in 2011 and 2012, it was noted that losses of otherwise available food might occur *after the food has been produced and made available for consumption*, most notably during distribution at the retail level.[43] A first step toward addressing this problem was taken in 2012, by introducing a parameter that captures food losses during distribution at the retail level. Region-specific values of average calorie losses have been estimated based on data provided in a recent FAO study of food losses,[44] ranging from 2 percent of the quantity distributed for dry grains, up to 10 percent for perishable products such as fresh fruit and vegetables.[45]

Estimating the coefficients of variation and skewness

Data from representative national household surveys are the only reliable source for directly estimating the other parameters of food consumption distributions.[46]

Different types of household survey, including income, expenditure and living standard measurement surveys, collect information on food acquisition (commonly referred to as "consumption" by economists). Their features and the quality of the information collected have implications for the estimates of habitual dietary energy consumption. In this connection, two main issues are noteworthy.

First, while undernourishment is considered an individual condition, data on food consumption are usually available only at the household level. Hence, individual food consumption can only be approximated by dividing available food by the number of household members.

Second, in most cases surveys collect data in terms of quantities of food acquired over a reference period. From these quantities, one needs to infer the levels of individual energy intake. The conversion of food quantities into dietary energy and making the distinction between acquisition and consumption often require large approximations. As these result in overestimation of the level of individual dietary energy intake in some cases and underestimation in others,[47] the simple sample variance of food consumption would not be a proper estimator of the variance of habitual food consumption in the population, which is needed to estimate of the CV of food consumption *of the representative individual*.

To control for such excessive variation in the data, in the past per capita caloric consumption figures were tabulated by household income class and the variation in average caloric consumption *between* income classes was calculated.[48] The resulting CV – labelled as "due to income" ($CV|y$) – excludes variability in habitual food consumption that is uncorrelated to household income. The "total" CV of habitual food consumption for the representative individual was then obtained using the following equation:

$$CV(x) = \sqrt{(CV|y)^2 + (CV|r)^2}$$

where $CV|r$ reflects variation caused by factors that induce variability in food consumption and are not correlated to income.[49] With the 2011–12 revision of the methodology, a more advanced method for estimating the CV and skewness in food consumption has been implemented. This is based on regression analysis that decomposes the total variation of food consumption into two components: one that reflects the variability of habitual food consumption and another that, due to the variability of observed consumption around its mean, is unrelated to the concept of food insecurity that informs the PoU estimator. Research is continuing within the FAO Statistics Division on how to decompose most effectively the total variation present in food consumption data from available surveys.

Estimating the MDER threshold

To calculate the minimum dietary energy requirement (MDER) threshold, FAO employs normative energy requirement standards based on the result of the joint FAO/WHO/UNU expert consultation that produced the most up-to-date reference for human energy requirements.[50] These standards are obtained by calculating the needs for basic metabolism (i.e. the energy expended by the human body in a state of rest) and multiplying the latter by a factor greater than one, to take into account the physical activity associated with a normal and active life (referred to as the PAL [physical activity level] index).

As individual metabolic efficiency and physical activity levels are variable within groups of the same age and sex, energy requirements can only be expressed as ranges for such groups. To derive the MDER threshold, the minimum of each range for adults and adolescents is specified on the basis of the distribution of ideal body weights and the midpoint of the values of the PAL index associated with sedentary lifestyle (1.55). The lowest body weight for a given height that is compatible with good health is estimated on the basis of the fifth percentile of the distribution of body mass indices in healthy populations.[51] Once the minimum requirement for each sex-age group has been established, the population-level MDER threshold is obtained as a weighted average, considering the relative frequency of individuals in each group as weights.

That the threshold is determined with reference to light physical activity (as normally associated with a sedentary lifestyle) does not negate the fact that the population also includes persons engaged in moderate and intense physical activity. It is just one

---

BOX A2.1

Early projections misjudged number of undernourished in 2009–10

In the early months of 2008, the FAO Food Price Index had reached a new and pronounced high. This food price crisis, coupled with what appeared to be a worldwide economic crisis, led to concerns that the number of food-insecure people in the world would increase substantially. FAO was put under considerable pressure to provide early estimates of what the likely impacts on undernourishment might be, before the actual data needed to inform the PoU estimate were available. In response to such pressure, new ad hoc methods to gauge the likely increase in the number of undernourished people were devised. In the 2008 edition of The State of Food Insecurity in the World,[1] FAO predicted an increase of 75 million undernourished people in 2008 (almost 9 percent of the last available figure), bringing the total to 913 million. These estimates assumed a rather pessimistic evolution of global food supply. The following year, a further increase of about 11 percent of the number of undernourished was foreseen. This was based on the prediction of a model developed by the United States Department of Agriculture and a bleak global macroeconomic outlook – shared by all major international organizations – that predicted reduced export growth and capital inflows in developing countries, assuming that the financial crisis would lower the availability of foreign direct investment, remittances and, possibly, official development assistance.

The 20 percent increase over the 848 million undernourished people estimated for 2003–05 meant that the number of hungry people in 2009 could have exceeded the one billion mark.

As actual data on food availability and utilization for 2007–09 become available, it also became evident that the worst-case predictions that had informed the 2009 and 2010 editions of The State of Food Insecurity in the World,[2] had not materialized. Estimates produced with the traditional methodology in 2010 put the figure for the number of undernourished for 2005–07 back to 847.5 million; this figure did not change by much the following year, when an estimate of 850 million was produced for the 2006–08 period, well below the 913 million estimate for 2008 issued two years earlier. It also started to become evident that both the food price spike of 2007–08 and the ensuing economic crisis had not been as dire as previously assumed, at least in much of the developing world. Moreover, the pass-through of international prices for primary food products to final consumer prices was much more muted than previously feared. Analysis of food price transmission from the international market to domestic markets shows that many, though not all, developing countries managed to shelter their consumers from the international food price hikes. And finally, many developing countries recovered quickly from the impacts of the global recession or were not much affected by the financial crisis that had engulfed many developed countries.

---

[1] FAO. 2008. The State of Food Insecurity in the World 2008: High food prices and food insecurity – threats and opportunities. Rome.
[2] FAO. 2009. The State of Food Insecurity in the World 2009: Economic crises – impacts and lessons learned. Rome; FAO and WFP. 2010. The State of Food Insecurity in the World 2010: Addressing food insecurity in protracted crises. Rome.

way to avoid overestimating food inadequacy when only food consumption levels are observed that cannot be individually matched to the varying requirements.

A frequent misconception when assessing food inadequacy based on observed food consumption data is to refer to the mid-point in the overall range of requirements (that is, with reference to a PAL of 1.85) as the threshold to identify inadequate energy consumption within the population. Unfortunately, such reasoning would lead to gross bias. To appreciate why, notice that even in groups composed of only well-nourished people, roughly half of these will have intake levels below mean requirements, as there will be people engaged in low physical activity. Using the mean requirement as a threshold would certainly produce an overestimate, as all adequately nourished individuals with less than average requirements would be misclassified as undernourished.[52]

The value of the MDER threshold for all monitored countries is updated by FAO every two years, based on regular revisions of the population assessments of the UN Population Division as well as data on population heights from various sources, most notably the *Monitoring and Evaluation to Assess and Use Results* of the *Demographic and Health Surveys* (MEASURE DHS) project coordinated by USAID (http://www.measuredhs.com). When data on population heights are not available, reference is made either to data on heights from countries where similar ethnicities prevails, or to models that use partial information to estimate heights for various sex and age classes.

What the PoU measures (and what it does not)

The terms "undernourishment" and "hunger" implicitly refer to situations of a *continued inability to obtain enough food*. Often, the FAO undernourishment figures have been interpreted as if they provided an indication on the broader concept of food insecurity. This is certainly misleading. Four points are worth highlighting in this context.

First of all, while there may be various ways to measure quantities of food, the FAO method is defined with respect to dietary *energy*. It is very likely that a diet that provides insufficient

energy also does not guarantee sufficient protein and micronutrient intake. The reverse, however, is not true, as there may be micronutrient deficiencies associated with energy-abundant diets. This means that the PoU estimates will not reflect the full extent of *malnutrition*, which is still an important dimension of food insecurity, as explained in the discussion on the suite of food security indicators presented in this report.

A related point concerns the fact that the term "undernourishment" as used in naming the indicator, being based on food "consumption" data, refers to *access* to food, rather than to its *utilization*. This has sometimes been an additional source of confusion.[53]

Moreover, it should be emphasized that the degree of inadequacy measured by the PoU is relative to the *habitual consumption level*. The PoU refers to the likely proportion of individuals in a population in such a condition *over the period covered by the assessment*. As data used to estimate average consumption are recorded with reference to one year, the indicator can only be interpreted as capturing the extent of *chronic* food deprivation. It does not reflect the effects of temporary food shortages or of short-lived crises, unless such crises have long-lasting effects on peoples' ability to access food. This also means that it does not capture, for example, the economic and social costs associated with food procurement, which may have a strong impact on the quality of life of people who are striving to maintain adequate dietary energy intake, even if they do not become undernourished.

Finally, as extensively explained in this annex, the PoU indicator only provides a measure of the likely prevalence of food deprivation *for the entire population, and not separately for different population groups*. The national figures published in this report cannot easily be disaggregated to provide a picture of the state of undernourishment for particular geographic areas or for socio-economic groups within a country.

An important consequence of all this is that, for a more complete description of the state of food insecurity, the PoU indicator should be complemented by other indicators. A broader suite of food security indicators, capturing the various facets of food insecurity in a country and within its population, would also allow decision-makers to design and implement more targeted policy measures. The second section of this report presents an initial attempt at defining such a suite.

Glossary of selected terms used in the report

Anthropometry. Use of human body measurements to obtain information about nutritional status.

Body mass index (BMI). The ratio of weight-for-height measured as the weight in kilograms divided by the square of height in metres.

Dietary energy intake. The energy content of food consumed.

Dietary energy requirement (DER). The amount of dietary energy required by an individual to maintain body functions, health and normal activity.

Dietary energy supply (DES). Food available for human consumption, expressed in kilocalories per person per day (kcal/person/day). At country level, it is calculated as the food remaining for human use after deduction of all non-food utilizations (i.e. food = production + imports + stock withdrawals – exports – industrial use – animal feed – seed – wastage – additions to stock). Wastage includes losses of usable products occurring along distribution chains from farm gate (or port of import) up to the retail level.

Dietary energy supply adequacy. Dietary energy supply as a percentage of the average dietary energy requirement.

Food insecurity. A situation that exists when people lack secure access to sufficient amounts of safe and nutritious food for normal growth and development and an active and healthy life. It may be caused by the unavailability of food, insufficient purchasing power, inappropriate distribution or inadequate use of food at the household level. Food insecurity, poor conditions of health and sanitation and inappropriate care and feeding practices are the major causes of poor nutritional status. Food insecurity may be chronic, seasonal or transitory.

Food security. A situation that exists when all people, at all times, have physical, social and economic access to sufficient, safe and nutritious food that meets their dietary needs and food preferences for an active and healthy life. Based on this definition, four food security dimensions can be identified: food availability, economic and physical access to food, food utilization and stability over time.

Hunger. In this report the term hunger is used as being synonymous with chronic undernourishment.

Kilocalorie (kcal). A unit of measurement of energy. One kilocalorie equals 1 000 calories. In the International System of Units (SI), the universal unit of energy is the joule (J). One kilocalorie = 4.184 kilojoules (kJ).

Macronutrients. In this document, the proteins, carbohydrates and fats that are available to be used for energy. They are measured in grams.

Malnutrition. An abnormal physiological condition caused by inadequate, unbalanced or excessive consumption of macronutrients and/or micronutrients. Malnutrition includes undernutrition and overnutrition as well as micronutrient deficiencies.

Micronutrients. Vitamins, minerals and certain other substances that are required by the body in small amounts. They are measured in milligrams or micrograms.

Minimum dietary energy requirement (MDER). In a specified age/sex category, the minimum amount of dietary energy per person that is considered adequate to meet the energy needs at a minimum acceptable BMI of an individual engaged in low physical activity. If referring to an entire population, the minimum energy requirement is the weighted average of the minimum energy requirements of the different age/sex groups. It is expressed as kilocalories per person per day.

Nutrition security. A situation that exists when secure access to an appropriately nutritious diet is coupled with a sanitary environment, adequate health services and care, in order to ensure a healthy and active life for all household members. Nutrition security differs from food security in that it also considers the aspects of adequate caring practices, health and hygiene in addition to dietary adequacy.

Nutrition-sensitive intervention. Interventions designed to address the underlying determinants of nutrition (which include household food security, care for mothers and children and primary health care services and sanitation) but not necessarily having nutrition as the predominant goal.

Nutritional status. The physiological state of an individual that results from the relationship between nutrient intake and requirements and from the body's ability to digest, absorb and use these nutrients.

Overnourishment. Food intake that is continuously in excess of dietary energy requirements.

Overnutrition. A result of excessive food intake relative to dietary nutrient requirements.

Overweight and obesity. Body weight that is above normal for height as a result of an excessive accumulation of fat. It is usually a manifestation of overnourishment. Overweight is defined as a BMI of more than 25 but less than 30 and obesity as a BMI of 30 or more.

Stunting. Low height for age, reflecting a sustained past episode or episodes of undernutrition.

Undernourishment. A state, lasting for at least one year, of inability to acquire enough food, defined as a level of food intake insufficient to meet dietary energy requirements. For the purposes of this report, hunger was defined as being synonymous with chronic undernourishment.

Undernutrition. The outcome of undernourishment, and/or poor absorption and/or poor biological use of nutrients consumed as a result of repeated infectious disease. It includes being underweight for one's age, too short for one's age (stunted), dangerously thin for one's height (wasted) and deficient in vitamins and minerals (micronutrient malnutrition).

Underweight. Low weight for age in children, and BMI of less than 18.5 in adults, reflecting a current condition resulting from inadequate food intake, past episodes of undernutrition or poor health conditions.

Wasting. Low weight for height, generally the result of weight loss associated with a recent period of starvation or disease.

1   Armenia, Azerbaijan, Cuba, Djibouti, Georgia, Ghana, Guyana, Kuwait, Kyrgyzstan, Nicaragua, Peru, Saint Vincent and the Grenadines, Samoa, Sao Tome and Principe, Thailand, Turkmenistan, Venezuela (Bolivarian Republic of) and Viet Nam.

2   FAO. 2009. *Declaration of the World Summit on Food Security.* Rome. 7 pp. (also available at ftp://ftp.fao.org/docrep/fao/Meeting/018/k6050e.pdf).

3   World Health Organization. 1995. *Physical status: the use and interpretation of anthropometry. Report of a WHO Expert Committee.* WHO Technical Report Series 854. Geneva, Switzerland (also available at http://whqlibdoc.who.int/trs/WHO_TRS_854.pdf).

4   FAO. 2010. *Global Forest Resources Assessment 2010: Main report.* FAO Forestry Paper 163. Rome.

5   Correlations were computed on panel data from 1996 to 2008 for all countries for which data were available, using Pearson's correlation coefficient (sigma two-tailed). Those quoted are statistically significant at the 1 percent level.

6   Data for 1990, 1993, 1996, 1999, 2002, 2005 and 2008 from POVCALNET, the online poverty analysis tool of the World Bank.

7   J. Rahman and A. Yusuf. 2010. *Economic growth in Bangladesh: experience and policy priorities* (available at http://www.hks.harvard.edu/fs/drodrik/Growth diagnostics papers/Economic growth in Bangladesh - experience and policy priorities.pdf).

8   W.M.H. Jaim and S. Akter. 2012. *Seed, fertilizer and innovation in Bangladesh: industry and policy issues for the future.* Project Paper. International Food Policy Research Institute and Cereal Systems Initiative for South Asia (available at http://www.ifpri.org/sites/default/files/publications/csisapp1.pdf).

9   National Food Policy Plan of Action and Country Investment Plan Monitoring Report (2012)

10 BRAC BCUP Sharecropper Development Programme.

11 E.M. Schmidt. 2012. The effect of women's intrahousehold bargaining power on child health outcomes in Bangladesh. *Undergraduate Economic Review,* 9(1): Article 4 (available at http://digitalcommons.iwu.edu/uer/vol9/iss1/4).

12 M.N. Begum and R.R. Sutradhar. 2012. *Behaviour of remittance inflows and its determinants in Bangladesh.* Bangladesh Bank Working Paper Series: WP1202. Dhaka, Bangladesh Bank.

13 H. Zillur Rahman and L.A. Choudhury. 2012. *Social safety nets in Bangladesh. Volume 2: Ground realities and policy challenges.* Dhaka, Power and Participation Research Centre and United Nations Development Programme.

14 UNDP/WFP/AusAID/DFID. 2012. *Report 1: Action plan for building a national social protection strategy mission on the Bangladesh National Social Protection Strategy (NSPS).*

15 IFAD. 2012. *Republic of Ghana. Country programme evaluation.* Rome.

16 World Bank, Danida and KfW. 2011. *Republic of Ghana: Joint review of public expenditure and financial management* (available at http://www.mofep.gov.gh/sites/default/files/reports/Review_of_Public_Expenditure_1011.pdf).

17 S. Asuming-Brempong. 2003. *Policy Module Ghana: Economic and agricultural policy reforms and their effects on the role of Agriculture in Ghana.* Paper prepared for the Roles of Agriculture International Conference, 20–22 October, Rome. Rome, FAO.

18 Overseas Development Institute. 2010. *Ghana's sustained agricultural growth: Putting underused resources to work.* London; and IFAD. 2012. *Republic of Ghana. Country Programme Evaluation.* Rome.

19 WFP. 2009. *Comprehensive food security and vulnerability analysis (CFSVA).* Ghana.

20 S.M. Sultan and T. Schrofer. 2008. *Building support to have targeted social protection interventions for the poorest – the case of Ghana.* Paper presented at the Conference on Social Protection for the Poorest in Africa: Learning from Experience, Entebbe, Uganda, 8–10 September 2008.

21 IMF. 2012. *Nepal 2012 Article IV Consultation.* IMF Country Report No.12/326. Washington, DC.

22 National Planning Commission and Central Bureau of Statistics. 2013. *Nepal thematic report on food security and nutrition 2013.* Kathmandu (also available at http://reliefweb.int/sites/reliefweb.int/files/resources/wfp256518.pdf).

23 WFP Nepal. 2010. *More than roads. Using markets to feed the hungry in Nepal.* Kathmandu.

24 Ministry of Health and Population, New ERA, and ICF International Inc. 2012. *Nepal demographic and health survey 2011.* Kathmandu, Nepal, and Calverton, Maryland, USA, Ministry of Health and Population, New ERA and ICF International.

25 WFP. 2009. *Evaluation of the effects of the global financial crisis at macro-level and on vulnerable households in Nicaragua.* Rome; RUTA. 2011. *Nicaragua: Caso de la experiencia del Bono Productivo Agropecuario* (available at http://www.ruta.org/Documentos-CD/ExpereinciasSistematizadas/PDF/NICARAGUA_CasoBonoProductivoAgropecuario.pdf).

26 R. Estrada. 2012. *Perfil de la pobreza rural en Nicaragua.* Rome, IFAD.

27 L. Knuth and M. Vidar. 2011. *Constitutional and legal protection of the Right to Food around the world.* Right to Food Studies series. Rome, FAO.

28 World Bank and Alliance for Global Justice. 2010. *The Global Justice Monitor,* May/June 2010.

29 World Bank. 2012. *Can small farmers protect themselves against bad weather?* From Evidence to Policy, Note 71392. Washington, DC.

30 Z. Lerman and D. Sedik. 2010. *The economic effects of land reform in Tajikistan.* Report prepared for the European Commission under the EC/FAO Food Security Programme – Phase II, Food Security Information for Action (available at ftp://ftp.fao.org/docrep/fao/011/aj285e/aj285e00.pdf).

31 K. Akramov and G. Shreedhar. 2012. *Economic development, external shocks, and food security in Tajikistan.* IFPRI Discussion Paper 01163. Washington, DC, International Food Policy Research Institute.

32 Tajikistan Living Standards Survey 2009; Akramov and Shreedhar (2012) (see note 31).

33 World Bank. 2011. *Uganda: Agriculture for inclusive growth in Uganda.* Washington, DC.

34 Ministry of Agriculture, Animal Industry and Fishery. 2010. *Agriculture sector development strategy and investment*

NOTES

plan: 2010/11 – 2014/15. Kampala; World Bank. 2010. *Uganda – Agriculture public expenditure review*. Washington, DC (available at https://openknowledge. worldbank.org/handle/10986/2910).

35 Monitoring African Food and Agriculture Policies. 2013. *Uganda: MAFAP Country Profile*. Rome, MAFAP.

36 WFP and Uganda Bureau of Statistics. 2013. *Comprehensive Food Security and Vulnerability Analysis: Uganda* (available at http://documents.wfp.org/stellent/ groups/public/documents/ena/ wfp256989.pdf).

37 Ministry of Finance, Planning and Economic Development. 2000. *Poverty reduction strategy paper. Uganda's Poverty Eradication Action plan summary and main objectives*. Kampala.

38 Uganda Bureau of Statistics. 2003. *UNHS 2002/03 report of the socio-economic survey*. Kampala.

39 FAO. 1963. *The Third World Food Survey*, pp. 39–40. Rome. The foundations of the methodology are to be found in: P.V. Sukhatme. 1961. The world's hunger and future needs in food supplies. *The Journal of the Royal Statistical Society, Series A (general)*, 124: 463–525. After its introduction in 1963, it was then used to produce estimates of the likely proportion of the population of several countries who were undernourished in 1969–71 and in 1972–74. These were published in: FAO. 1977. *The Fourth World Food Survey*. Rome (Appendix M, pp. 127–128). Revised regional and global estimates were then published for 1969–71 and 1979–81 in: FAO. 1985. *The Fifth World Food Survey*. Rome (Table 3.1, pp. 22–23). Further revised regional and global estimates were presented for 1969–71, 1979–81 and 1990–92 in: FAO. 1996. *The Sixth World Food Survey*. Rome (Table 14, p. 45, and Appendix 3, pp. 114–43). Since 1999, estimates at country level, in addition to regional and global figures, have been published annually in *The State of Food Insecurity in the World*.

40 See, FAO (1996, Appendix 3, pp. 114–43) (see note 39), and L. Naiken. 2003. FAO methodology for estimating the prevalence of undernourishment. In: *Measurement and assessment of food deprivation and undernutrition. International Scientific Symposium, FAO, Rome, 26–28 June 2002* (available at http://www.fao.org/docrep/005/Y4249E/ y4249e00.htm).

41 Even just the actual basal metabolic rate, arguably the largest contributor to normal energy requirements in humans, is difficult to assess at the individual level and at reasonable cost.

42 A. Azzalini. 1985. A class of distributions which includes the normal ones. *Scandinavian Journal of Statistics,* 12: 171–178.

43 Such losses have been identified as a possible source of bias in FAO estimates of undernourishment using the food balance sheets' DES to estimate mean food consumption. See R. Sibrián, J. Komoroska and J. Mernies. 2006. *Estimating household and institutional food wastage and losses: Measuring food deprivation and food excess in the total population*. FAO Statistics Division Working Paper Series No. ES/ESSA/001e. Rome.

44 FAO. 2011. *Global food losses and food waste: Extent, causes and prevention*, by J. Gustavsson, C. Cederberg, U. Sonesson, R. van Otterdijk and A. Meybeck. Rome.

45 FAO, IFAD and WFP. 2012. *The State of Food Insecurity in the World 2012: Economic growth is necessary but not sufficient to accelerate reduction of hunger and malnutrition*. Rome, FAO.

46 When no data on the distribution of actual food consumption are available, parameters related to the variability of food access have been estimated based on the distribution of food expenditures, on the inequality of income distribution or, in the worst case, on child mortality rates. See Naiken (2003, pp. 14 and 15) (see note 40).

47 It is not uncommon to observe values lower than 800 kcal or in excess of 5 000 kcal, clearly unreliable measures of habitual daily caloric consumption.

48 This was obtained by calculating the CV, assigning to each individual a level of dietary energy consumption equal to the median value of per capita dietary energy consumption recorded among the households grouped in the same income class.

49 See Naiken (2003) pp. 13 and 14) (see note 40).

50 FAO, WHO and UNU. 2004. *Human Energy Requirements. Report of a Joint FAO/WHO/UNI Expert Consultation, Rome 17–24 October 2001*. Food and Nutrition Technical Report Series No. 1. Rome, FAO.

51 For a detailed description of the procedure, see Naiken (2003) (see note 40).

52 The point was effectively made by P.V. Sukhatme in 1960 (see note 39), and subsequently recognized, among others, by Srinivasan in 1981; see T.N. Srinivasan. Malnutrition: some measurement and policy issues. *Journal of Development Economics*, 8(1): 3–19. Yet, researchers have persisted in making such a mistake in later years (for example, see L. Smith, H. Alderman and D. Aduayom. 2006. *Food insecurity in sub-Saharan Africa: new estimates from household expenditure surveys*. IFPRI Research Report 146. Washington DC, IFPRI.

53 "Nourishing" here must be taken to mean "providing with food", and is not related to the actual nutrition conditions. A less appealing alternative to "undernourishment" could be "underfeeding", which might have the advantage of not creating the false expectation that the indicator is capturing the state of malnutrition resulting from inadequate absorption of nutrients. In languages other than English, such as French, the difference is clearer, as there are distinct terms to refer to "feeding" ("*alimentation*") as opposed to "nourishing" ("*nutrition*"). The correct term for the FAO indicator in French is, in fact, "*prevalence de la sous-alimentation*" rather than "*prevalence de la sous-nutrition*".